**INSIGHT FROM GOD'S WORD
ON 12 *BURNING* ISSUES**

Compiled by
Rick Bundschuh

Edited by
Annette Parrish

Illustrated by
Tom Finley

Regal Books

A Division of GL Publications
Ventura, California, U.S.A.

Published by Regal Books
A Division of GL Publications
Ventura, California 93006
Printed in U.S.A.

The authors and publisher have sought to locate and secure permission to reprint copyrighted materials in this book. If any such acknowledgments have been omitted, the publisher would appreciate receiving the information so that proper credit may be given in future printings.

The publishers do not necessarily endorse the entire contents of all publications referred to in this book.

Scripture taken from the HOLY BIBLE: NEW INTERNATIONAL VERSION. Copyright © 1973, 1978, 1984 by the International Bible Society. Used by permission of Zondervan Bible Publishers. Also quoted is *NASB—The New American Standard Bible,* copyright © The Lockman Foundation 1960, 1962, 1968, 1971, 1972, 1973, 1975. Used by permission.

Library of Congress Cataloging-in-Publication Data

Hot Buttons II.

   "The Light Force."
   Contents: AIDS / Todd Temple—Trauma in the home / Jim Burns—Living together (without benefit of marriage) / Rick Bundschuh—[etc.]
    1. Youth—Religious life. 2. Youth—Conduct of life. [1. Christian life] I. Bundschuh, Rick, 1951- . II. Parrish, Annette. III. Finley, Tom, 1951- ill.
BV4531.2. H593   1987   248.8'3   87-7226
ISBN 0-8307-1221-6

3 4 5 6 7 8 9 10 / 91 90 89

Rights for publishing this book in other languages are contracted by Gospel Literature International (GLINT) foundation. GLINT also provides technical help for the adaptation, translation, and publishing of Bible study resources and books in scores of languages worldwide. For further information, contact GLINT, Post Office Box 488, Rosemead, California, 91770, U.S.A., or the publisher.

Contents

AIDS: What Teenagers Should Know About It

Todd Temple

The Christian singer pauses between songs. Blocking the stage lights from his eyes, he looks out on a thousand faces to explain that the next song speaks of God's judgment against sin. The audience is silent. He points out that every sin has its price. "Amen!" someone shouts from the crowd. "Sinful actions will be judged!" (More amens.) "And upon the wicked practices of homosexuals," he continues with vehemence, "God's judgment is AIDS!" Overwhelming applause. Ironically, some of the individuals clapping are carrying the AIDS virus and don't even know it. Yet.

Colleen, 19, is sitting in the front row. She got the virus three years ago by having sex with the guy she was dating. (He got it from sex with an old girlfriend—who picked it up from a dirty needle the only time she ever tried speed.) Colleen has been having sex with her steady boyfriend, Roger, and now he is carrying the virus. Roger is sitting next to her in the crowd.

Phil and Vanessa are sitting a few rows behind them; they're married—and carry the AIDS virus. Vanessa was a virgin when they got married, but Phil had slept with a girl in high school whose old boyfriend was Haitian (he had received it from a contaminated needle at a health clinic there). Phil and Vanessa left their two-year-old son Michael with a baby-sitter tonight—Michael got the AIDS virus in his mother's womb.

John is sitting with a bunch of friends from his youth group. Tonight they are celebrating his fifteenth birthday—a significant event because he almost didn't live that long. Eight months ago he was hit by a car as he rode his bike home from school, and only through major blood transfusions were the doctors able to keep him alive through the emergency surgery. Some of the blood he received was tainted by the AIDS virus.

Not one of these AIDS virus carriers is homosexual, nor has any one of them ever had a homosexual experience. But in the next four years or so, some of them will develop Acquired Immune Deficiency Syndrome— AIDS—and they'll have learned too late that the virus is no respecter of sexual orientation. Even those who don't develop the disease themselves will pass the virus on to others, who will pass it on to still others. The results are sickening: of those who receive the AIDS virus, between one-fourth and one-half will eventually develop the AIDS disease. Death is almost certain.

AIDS is not a homosexual disease. The sexual habits of homosexual men make them more efficient transmitters of the virus, and so 65 percent of the known cases in the United States are homosexual men. But one-fourth of the cases are intravenous drug users, and one out of every ten victims got the virus through heterosexual sex, blood transfusion, an infected mother, or some undetermined method.[1]

Despite these facts, the Christian community has reacted to AIDS with energy unmatched. Preachers, musicians, and writers declare the disease as God's righteous judgment on homosexual sin. AIDS is the consequence for *Them*—the gays, the bisexuals, the sexually perverse. *They* deserve it. *They* reap what *They* sow. Romans 1:26,27 is often used to justify this view of AIDS:

> Because of this, God gave them over to shameful lusts. Even their women exchanged natural relations for unnatural ones. In the same way the men also abandoned natural relations with women and were inflamed with lust for one another. Men committed indecent acts with other men, and received in themselves the due penalty for their perversion.

AIDS, many claim, is the "due penalty for their perversion." At first look, it seems that they are absolutely right. But a careful reading of the Scripture shows otherwise.

The verses mention male and female homosexuals. Yet very few lesbians have AIDS. Does God practice sex discrimination by withholding women from judgment? And what about Colleen, Roger, Phil, Vanessa, Michael, John, and the hundreds of other young people who aren't homosexuals but have the "punishment"? Paul describes the penalty as a consequence that is unavoidable, and is assessed because of immoral sexual conduct. How is it that some unrepentant homosexuals are not being punished while blood recipients and children born to AIDS carriers are dying from the disease? If God is passing out AIDS as the punishment for homosexuals, He is getting some of the names mixed up.

Homosexual behavior is not the latest fad in sexual trends—it is as old as recorded history. Yet the first confirmed cases of AIDS did not occur until the late seventies. If this is the punishment Paul referred to 19 centuries ago, God has taken His time in dishing out the penalty.

Many other diseases and medical problems tend to attack a particular segment of society: sickle cell anemia occurs predominantly among blacks; Tay-Sachs disease primarily affects Eastern European Jews; ten times as many men as women have color blindness. Are these groups being singled out for special punishment? Maybe acne is God's punishment to adolescents, diaper rash His penalty for the childish behavior of infants, and constipation His judgment against old people who drive slowly.

In a way, all of these conditions are a part of God's judgment of a sinful world. Sin entered the world when Adam and Eve rebelled against God—the consequence was banishment from the garden, and the reality of pain, disease, and death. And since we have done no better than those two when it comes down to obedience to God, we are partly to blame for the evil around us.

AIDS is not necessarily God's special, divine judgment on homosexuals. However, like all diseases that are primarily transmitted through sex, it can be the consequence of wrong choices. But if AIDS isn't the judgment Paul mentions, what is? The Scripture states that there is a specific penalty for homosexual behavior and that offenders receive the penalty "in themselves." Sin in all its forms changes us on the *inside*—it alters our self-image, destroys our self-control, and drives a wedge between us and God. I believe the consequence of homosexual sin is the loss of sexual identity. The more homosexual experiences one has, the more severe the damage. Some individuals have so lost this identity they believe that they are men trapped in female bodies, or women trapped in male bodies. And pathetically, a few disfigure these bodies, attempting to make their outsides match up with the distorted images they have on the inside. This loss of sexual identity, along with the rest of the changes that take place in one's "self" as a result of sin, are penalties far worse than any disease: AIDS kills the body, but sin and its consequences kill the soul.

AIDS is the leprosy of the modern age. Imagine being such a "leper." It's cold season, and you pick up one like you do every year. Only this time you don't shake it off in a few days; instead, it just keeps getting worse. Your doctor discovers a mild pneumonia; you're to stay in bed for a week and take antibiotics. Two weeks later you're not any worse—but not any better, either. You check into the hospital so that a trained medical staff can give you intravenous treatment and monitor your improvement. But for two more weeks all they can monitor is your decline. Your body doesn't seem to respond to the antibiotics, so a series of blood tests are taken. Then the doctor tells you why you haven't been getting any better.

There's a problem in your body's natural protection system, which was supposed to fight off the pneumonia virus. Since the cold weakened your body, the virus was able to infect your lungs. But your immune system, fighting alongside the antibiotics, should have destroyed the enemy within the week. As it turned out, your antibodies never even showed up for the battle. The "command" cells (known as helper T cells) that were supposed to tell the antibodies where to go were destroyed by another virus that you've been carrying around for four years without knowing it. And since that virus (called HTLV-3) attacked the very cells that are in the business of killing viruses, your body is defenseless—a country without an army. In other words, you have AIDS.

Once you are diagnosed with the disease, your family and friends disappear; the fear of contamination taints every relationship. Those who do come into your room—doctors and nurses—speak through masks and touch with gloved hands. Like other terminally-ill patients, you sense that the hospital staff and volunteers don't want to grow too attached to you; it will be easier on them when you die if they lose a patient rather than a friend. When your roommate and other AIDS patients begin to die off, you realize that the only way out of this hospital ward is in a hearse. You are a modern-day leper, and nothing short of a miracle is going to keep you from dying as one.

Christ's treatment of the lepers is far different from the way we treat the similar outcasts of our day:

> A man with leprosy came to him and begged him on his knees, "If you are willing, you can make me clean." Filled with compassion, Jesus reached out his hand and touched the man. "I am willing," he said. "Be clean!" Immediately the leprosy left him and he was cured. Mark 1:40-42

Christ looked beyond the decaying flesh to find a soul desperate for the touch of another human. This one act of compassion ought to make us ashamed of our selfishness toward the untouchable human beings in our own society. Because of our judgmental reaction to the AIDS crisis, Christians have given the victims a view of our Lord that is the antithesis of His true nature. We portray Him as an angry God who strikes down sinners with a deadly virus. But He reveals Himself in Scripture as a loving God who allowed His own son to be struck down to save those sinners. Rose Hernandez, a hospital nurse working with AIDS victims in the San Francisco Bay area, describes her first encounter with an AIDS patient:

> Our head nurse said we would draw straws to see who would treat him because we were all making excuses for not wanting to become involved. I thought of the man's dignity and I volunteered to take care of him, remembering that the Lord was taking care of me. I was frightened. I wore double gloves, mask, gown, booties, and hat. The patient was about 23 years old, of Haitian background. I remember the tears in his eyes as I held his hand in my gloved hand. He wanted to be accepted, to die with dignity. I asked myself, "How can I judge these people?"[2]

As Christians, we need to stop using our knowledge of the Bible to find proof of God's judgment on sin. Instead, let's use it to show people that Christ's love is greater than sin and disease. Ray Stedman, pastor and popular Bible teacher, puts it this way: "The world says to the victim of AIDS, 'You made your bed, now lie in it,' but Jesus' words to him are, 'Rise, take up your bed and walk.'"[3]

As Christians, we can make a difference in the AIDS crisis by living out what Jesus would want us to do in the face of such a dark situation. Here are some ways teenagers can do that right now.

Deal in Compassion

In Matthew 25, Jesus tells a story of a group of people who, during their lives, fed the hungry, satisfied the thirsty, gave comfort to strangers, clothed the needy, and visited the sick and imprisoned. He explains to His listeners that whenever they did these things for anyone, they were doing them for Him. Jesus implies that whenever we visit the sick, we visit Him. There are few people sicker than an AIDS victim, and no one more worthy of our time than the God who created him.

Feeling hopelessly rejected, many AIDS patients long to know that they are loved by someone. Some teenagers have befriended patients, coming to visit them each week. These young people sit and chat, pray, or just hold hands—and show in their actions that Christ's love is real. Youth groups run errands and do chores for those too sick to do these tasks on their own. Many Christian victims who have been rejected by their own churches have found comfort in the Christian love demonstrated by these high schoolers. And many other victims have been so struck with the compassion of these students that they have turned their lives over to Christ.

Many otherwise compassionate people are hesitant to get involved with AIDS patients for fear of contracting the disease themselves. The risk is much smaller than many realize. The AIDS virus is very fragile outside the human body, usually dying within seconds of being exposed to the air. Basic sanitary precautions should be taken: avoid contact with body fluids and open wounds, and wash your hands after touching the patient. Always talk to the patient's doctor to find out if there are any extra precautions you should take. By finding out the facts, fear won't keep you from touching the life of someone who needs you.

Stop the Suffering

You can keep others from getting AIDS by knowing the facts and telling others. Most high schoolers are dangerously ignorant to the deadliness of AIDS. A survey of 1,332 students in San Francisco showed that forty percent didn't know that AIDS is incurable.[4] And since San Francisco has the second highest AIDS victim population in the country, these students are probably better educated than most. Here are some facts to help you teach your friends.

At the time of this writing there is still no cure for AIDS, and no vaccine to prevent others from becoming victims. Drugs being tested now have shown some promise in prolonging lives, but they work with only some strains of the disease, and they don't reverse the damage already done. Most of the people carrying the virus in their bodies don't know it since it takes up to five years for symptoms to appear. That means they will probably spread the disease to others. One AIDS researcher estimates that by 1991, the virus will be present in the blood of between 5 million and 10 million Americans— staggering numbers when you realize that up to half of them could develop the disease and die.[5]

By the end of 1986, an estimated 1.5 million Americans carried the AIDS virus in their bodies, 29,000 had contracted the disease, and 18,000 of these had already died from it. America is getting off easy when you look at the AIDS epidemic in central Africa. As many as 5 million are carrying the virus, and leading AIDS researchers estimate the death toll so far at several hundred thousand. And in Africa, the disease kills as many women as it does men. AIDS is an international tragedy.

Let friends know that AIDS is spreading fast. Let them know that one doesn't have to be a homosexual or an intravenous drug user to get it. Tell them that when you have sex with someone, you are having sex with everyone your partner has had sex with in the past decade. AIDS is going to be with us for a long time, but you can save lives by knowing the facts and telling others what you know.

Practice Forgiveness

Because most of the AIDS victims in this country are homosexuals, most conversations on the subject eventually move on to discussions about homosexuality. For some reason, Christians have taken this particular sin and drawn more attention to it than just about any other sin common to man—and it's not as if there aren't any other sins to choose from. In fact, the Bible says that we have all chosen sins of our own to commit. Then it gets worse. Romans 6:23 points out that our own sins are worthy of the penalty of death. Apparently, God doesn't grade sins on a curve: Lying—C; Fornication—D+; Homosexuality—F. Life is a Pass-or-Fail course, and all of us have flunked.

The great news of the gospel is that we can be forgiven of our sins and the grade book thrown away. This is true for *anyone* in the class, regardless of what it was they did to fail the class in the first place. God is ready to forgive your sins—are you willing to forgive those whose sins make headlines more than yours?

The AIDS crisis has put Christians at the crossroads; the world is waiting to see which road we take. Will we allow millions to die while we applaud it as God's justice for sinners? Or will we reach out in the name of Christ and love those He chose to die for? Watch your step.

Questions and Answers About Aids[6,7]

What does AIDS stand for?	Acquired Immune Deficiency Syndrome
What is AIDS?	A fatal disease that attacks the immune system, leaving the victim's body defenseless to illnesses that it can normally fight off such as pneumonia and meningitis.
How do you get AIDS?	Mostly by having sex with an infected person or by sharing needles and syringes used to inject illegal drugs. The virus is present in the blood, semen, and vaginal secretions. It can be transmitted from one homosexual partner to another, or from a man to a woman or a woman to a man during sexual intercourse or oral sex. The virus can enter the body through sores in the mouth and microscopic tears in the tissue of sex organs.
How else is AIDS transmitted?	Some victims were exposed to the AIDS virus through blood they have received in a transfusion. Since the start of careful blood

screening tests, this rarely occurs now. About a third of the babies born to mothers with AIDS are infected.

Can you get AIDS from shaking hands, hugging, kissing, coughing, sneezing, or eating food prepared by someone with AIDS? Can you get it through masturbation, toilet seats, door knobs, or insect bites?

No known cases have been transmitted in any of these ways.

Can you get AIDS by having your ears pierced?

No one is known to have received it this way as yet, but it is conceivable. If you are having this done, insist on a sterile needle.

Can you get AIDS from someone who doesn't know he or she has it?

Yes. This is usually what happens. Because it sometimes takes five years (and possibly longer) after exposure for symptoms to appear, most carriers don't discover they have it until they have already passed it on.

Can you be infected with the AIDS virus and

Yes. Between one-fourth and one-half of those infected with the virus will develop AIDS within

never get AIDS?	four to ten years. Some say that the percentage is more like one-half to two-thirds.
How can I protect myself from getting AIDS?	Wait until marriage before having sex. When you have sex with someone, you are having sex with everyone he or she has had sex with for the past 10 years.
Where can I find out more about AIDS?	Your local Red Cross office carries information, as do local and state health departments.

NOTES

1. Kathleen McAuliffe, "AIDS: At the Dawn of Fear," *U.S. News & World Report,* January 12, 1987, p. 66.
2. Ray Stedman, "A Christian Response to the AIDS Issue" [seminar held at Peninsula Bible Church, Palo Alto, California, December 8, 1985].
3. Ibid.
4. McAuliffe, "AIDS," p. 68.
5. Tom Morganthan, "Future Shock," *Newsweek,* November 24, 1986. [Interview of Dr. Robert Redfield, infectious disease specialist, Walter Reed Army Medical Center].
6. McAuliffe, "AIDS," p. 66.
7. C. Everett Koop, "AIDS: The Surgeon General's Report on Acquired Immune Deficiency Syndrome," *Los Angeles Times,* December 7, 1986, pp. 1-8.

Trauma in the Home: Victims of Abuse

Jim Burns

The odds are that you or a close friend of yours has been a victim of "trauma in the home." Let's face it, today's home is not always a happy place. Thousands of people suffer in silence. Others may tell their friends about the difficult times they are experiencing. Some express their suffering through angry or self-destructive behavior. Still others suffer physical, verbal, or emotional abuse and yet fail to recognize that they are victims of abuse.

Did you know you are a victim of abuse if someone close to you is an alcoholic, a drug abuser, or has mental or emotional problems? Sexual abuse and physical abuse also produce trauma in the home and cause a person to become a victim.

A recent University of Rhode Island study showed that the greatest place of violence in the United States is the home. If you have not experienced some form of trauma in your home, consider yourself one of the very fortunate people in the world. You can read this chapter in order to be better prepared to help a hurting friend. If stress, abuse, and trauma have been a part of your life, there is hope and there are positive solutions to your family situation.

Are You a Victim?

Jill's father drank too much. Most of the time he was under control, but every once in a while he would get totally out-of-control drunk. His abusive language and embarrassing behavior caused Jill to be fearful of her father. She spent her high school days trying to please her dad and trying to get the encouragement and love she seldom received from him.

In high school Jill became extremely sexually promiscuous and started the compulsive behavior of overeating. She also overspent on her frequent shopping sprees. Jill is a victim of trauma in the home.

Tom's mother had major emotional problems. Her own childhood was a disaster. She was pushing the divorce rate higher since she was leaving her fourth husband and moving rapidly toward marrying number five. Tom was in his junior year of high school. His mother's verbal slashings, extreme moodiness, and plain old weird behavior were really doing a number on Tom's emotional, physical and spiritual life. He loved his mother—yet hated her behavior. He was often depressed, withdrawn, and felt guilty about his dislike for his family. He entered the military the day he was eligible in order to flee the trauma of his home. Tom is a victim of emotional abuse.

It seemed so innocent when it first started. Sherri's father began to rub her back. Then his hands moved from her back to her more private areas. Before she knew what was actually happening to her, he was forcing her to have sexual intercourse with him. Sherri had always adored her father. She trusted him. She loved and respected him. Four years after the first sex act with him and many sexual encounters later, she was numb, sick, disgusted, and contemplating suicide. Sherri is a victim of sexual abuse.

There are thousands, perhaps millions, of victims of trauma in the home. Each story is a personal tragedy. Each story is complicated and has no easy answers. If you are a victim, your story may not be as tragic as the ones I've mentioned, or, you may identify closely to Jill, Tom, or Sherri. But no matter what your trauma or abusive situation, you are a victim.

What do I mean by a victim? I mean a person who is in a relationship with someone whose sickness affects his or her life in a major, negative way. Jill, Tom, and Sherri's stories illustrate the principle that you can't be the child of an alcoholic and be unaffected or go through the divorce of your parents unscathed. No one who has been sexually, physically, or emotionally abused is not a victim. But you may be a victim of abuse without having ever thought of it before in those terms.

People react to their negative home circumstances with all kinds of different behaviors. Jill was raised in the church but rebelled against God and was heavily involved in the party scene. Tom ran away from his problems. He was known as the class clown. He was hiding his hurt behind a phoney smile. Sherri became the leader of her church's youth group. She shared her hurts and doubts with no one. She was a perfectionist. Her perfect behavior was a way of coping with the abusive situation at home. The longer she repressed her hurt, the deeper the scars grew.

If you have identified yourself as a victim or if you view your own home situation as less than perfect, then you should know that *there is hope.* If you are not a victim, but one of your friends is experiencing trauma in the home, then you can help guide him towards hope and healing and away from his world of hurt and distrust.

Positive Solutions for Negative Home Situations

Realize and accept the fact that it is not your fault.

Far too many people blame themselves for their loved one's sickness. When Tom's parents divorced, he blamed himself. He told me that if he and his sister didn't argue so much his mom and dad wouldn't have split up. Tom needed to know he was not responsible for his father's and mother's problems.

Sherri believed she must have subconsciously been flirting with her father to lead him on sexually. Sherri's father is sick. It was not her fault. She was a victim of his illness.

We can all blame ourselves for most any trauma we experience. But one of the first steps toward wholeness is to quit blaming ourselves. Let the person with the abusive behavior take responsibility for his or her actions.

Seek help. Don't suffer in silence.

Perhaps the most important step toward a healthy life for a victim is to seek help. Sometimes seeking help is embarrassing; other times the victim may feel disloyal for revealing a deep, dark family secret. But the truth is, the family suffering trauma needs help in order to get better. Someone must be the one to seek that help.

The thousands of people who choose to suffer in silence are choosing to get worse and not better. When a person has been abused, he or she is likely to become sick also. Hurts cannot be wished away.

Victims are often surprised to find that they are not the only ones who have suffered their particular brand of trauma. Help is available through trusted friends and qualified counselors.

It is helpful to know that counselors do not talk to others about what their clients tell them. This rule comes under their code of professional ethics. What their clients tell them is called "privileged information."

Jill confided to her youth pastor that her father's alcohol problem was not only his personal problem but had also become the whole family's problem. She realized her sensual, party behavior was getting her into trouble and causing deep-rooted unhappiness. Her youth pastor met with her regularly and got her involved in an Alateen support group in her community. Jill's progress was remarkable and swift. If she had waited to seek help it would have taken longer to correct her own destructive behavior. It does not matter if Jill's father never changes; that is beyond Jill's control. She needed to seek help in order to prevent herself from taking a similar tumultuous path. Seek help. Please don't suffer alone.

God cares. He really does!

Frankly, most people I know who have experienced trauma in the home struggle with their relationship with God. It is difficult for them to view Him as the loving God He is.

Some victims have a difficult time comprehending the

unconditional, sacrificial love that Jesus Christ has for them. Yet it is true that God loves each of us unconditionally. His deep love has no strings attached. He loves us not for what we do but simply for who we are: His children. God is a loving Father. Even if you personally have not experienced a loving father, you must look beyond your own personal circumstances to the actions of God throughout history.

I believe that Jesus Christ would have suffered on the cross if you were the only person in the world. Paul described it this way: "God demonstrates his own love toward us, in that while we were yet sinners, Christ died for us" (Rom. 5:8).

If God loves you enough to allow His only Son, Jesus, to die for you, then I believe He also cares deeply about you and your home life. I've seen tragic lives restored to wholeness because people allowed God to reconstruct their past and fill their future with hope. I'm afraid too many people spend their energy blaming God instead of being comforted by Him. God wants to walk with you through your valley of hurt and disappointment. King David of the Old Testament had the right attitude when he wrote the famous words we know as Psalm 23:

> The Lord is my shepherd, I shall not be in want.
> He makes me lie down in green pastures, he leads me beside quiet waters, he restores my soul.
> He guides me in paths of righteousness for his name's sake.
> Even though I walk through the valley of the shadow of death, I will fear no evil, for you are with me; your rod and your staff, they comfort me.

You prepare a table before me in the presence
of my enemies.
You anoint my head with oil; my cup overflows.
Surely goodness and love will follow me all the
days of my life, and I will dwell in the house of
the Lord forever.

Some people need to understand that their circumstances may never change, but their attitude can change and that makes all the difference in the world.

I love the thoughts expressed by an unknown author and simply entitled "Footprints."

One night a man had a dream. He dreamed he
was walking along the beach with the Lord.
Across the sky flashed scenes from his life. For
each scene, he noticed two sets of footprints in
the sand: one belonged to him, and the other to
the Lord.

When the last scene of his life flashed before
him, he looked back at the footprints in the
sand. He noticed that many times along the
path of his life there was only one set of footprints. He also noticed that it happened at the
very lowest and saddest times in his life.

This really bothered him and he questioned the
Lord about it. "Lord, you said that once I
decided to follow you, you'd walk with me all
the way. But I have noticed that during the
most troublesome times in my life, there is only
one set of footprints. I don't understand why

when I needed you most you would leave me."

The Lord replied, "My precious, precious child, I love you and would never leave you. During the times of trial and suffering, when you see only one set of footprints, it was then that I carried you."

If you have experienced trauma in your home, you can take charge of the battle for your own recovery. The choices can be yours. You can overcome your pain.

The decision to move toward wholeness is not always easy, but it is always the best. The question I leave with you is: who and where do you want to be in 10 years? The decisions you make today will affect you the rest of your life. Choose health and wholeness and remember, God walks with you through your darkest times.

Comfort for Those Who Are Suffering

There are over 3000 promises made by God in the Bible. The following are some of the promises that may be very comforting for those suffering trauma in the home.

Theme	Promise
Love	*Though the mountains be shaken and the hills be removed, yet my unfailing love for you will not be shaken nor my covenant of peace be removed, says the Lord, who has compassion on you.* Isaiah 54:10

For God so loved the world that he gave his one and only Son, that whoever believes in him shall not perish but have eternal life. John 3:16

Forgiveness

If we confess our sins, he is faithful and just and will forgive us our sins and purify us from all unrighteousness. 1 John 1:9

All the prophets testify about him that everyone who believes in him receives forgiveness of sins through his name. Acts 10:43

Comfort

But from everlasting to everlasting the Lord's love is with those who fear him, and his righteousness with their children's children. Psalm 103:17

And surely I am with you always, to the very end of the age. Matthew 28:20

Guidance

But the Counselor, the Holy Spirit, whom the Father will send in my name, will teach you all things and will remind you of everything I have said to you. John 14:26

But when he, the Spirit of truth, comes, he will guide you into all truth. He will not speak on his own; he will speak only what he hears, and he will tell you what is yet to come. John 16:13

Joy

Nehemiah said, "Go and enjoy choice food and sweet drinks, and send some to those who have nothing prepared. This day is sacred to our Lord. Do not grieve, for the joy of the Lord is your strength. Nehemiah 8:10

Until now you have not asked for anything in my name. Ask and you will receive, and your joy will be complete. John 16:24

Guilt   *In him and through faith in him we may approach God with freedom and confidence.* Ephesians 3:12

If you, O Lord, kept a record of sins, O Lord, who could stand? But with you there is forgiveness; therefore you are feared. Psalm 130:3,4

Help!

If you or someone you know is suffering, you can draw courage from the fact that there is help available through church, government, and non-profit organizations. Here is a list of ideas for places you can go to for help.

- Church staff—your pastor, youth pastor, or other trusted member of the church staff.
- A church-related counseling center.
- Your school counselor.
- Hotlines—Call 411 and ask for the number of the specific hotline you need. Many communities have crisis, rape, and suicide prevention counselors available over the phone.

- For alcoholism—Alcoholics Anonymous, Alateen, Alanon.
- For drug abuse—Narcotics Anonymous.
- For a comprehensive list of services in your area, call your local Public Health Services or Public Social Services.
- Look in the phone book under the government (county or city) listings for ideas for other service agencies.

Living Together (Without Benefit of Marriage)

Rick Bundschuh

Spin your imagination dial back to somewhere in the third grade. Imagine a grimy-faced kid unconditionally giving you a cool yo-yo that lights up and whistles as it spins. Imagine that the next day he comes back and demands you return *his* yo-yo. Picture him yelling and screaming and finally running to get a teacher when you say, "Give it back? No way! It's mine. You gave it to me."

Do you remember what little kids call a person who gives someone something and then goes back on the deal? They call him an "Indian giver." I'm not sure if the term reflected the actions of a few corrupt Indians in the Old West or if it is a description of how some government officials broke promises made to the Indians. But either way, in "kid-dom" Indian giver was one of the worst things you could be called. Calling a person an Indian giver is a little kid's way of pointing out someone who breaks promises or, more specifically, takes away what they had once given.

All little kids have an innate knowledge that you shouldn't be the kind of person who gives something and then takes it away. No kid in his right mind would make any kind of a deal with a person who might at any time reclaim his property and go home. Yet adults sometimes fall prey to Indian givers in a very important area of their lives. They do this when they choose to live with a member of the opposite sex without benefit of marriage. People who choose to live together rather than make a life commitment are Indian givers when it comes to human relationships.

Christians agree that it is against God's moral law to live together on a trial basis. Yet it is surprising just how many people who claim to be Christians try to find some way to justify or excuse why they happen to be living with their boyfriends or girlfriends.

In the following pages you will find some very strong arguments against living together. While a few of the arguments apply only to people who are Christians, many of the others apply to anyone with just an ounce of common sense.

People who live together instead of marrying generally give the same few reasons for their life-style. Let's examine these reasons to see if they make sense and if they are really good for those involved and for the society in which we live.

It is very important to understand that people will often fire off *all* of these reasons in one blast if they feel someone is being critical of their living arrangement. Most of the time, especially after a bit of conversation, *one* of the following reasons will bob to the surface as the true rationale for their behavior. The rest are merely smoke screens or diversionary tactics to take the heat of battle away from a guilty conscience.

Reason 1
We don't need a piece of paper to show that we love each other

This line of reasoning sounds very noble, even a touch romantic. There is a streak of rebellion in it also. Most people who use this line will swear up and down that they are genuinely and permanently committed to the person with whom they are living. They just don't see the legal formalities as being important.

Actually this argument contains a kernel of truth and that is what makes it so appealing. It is valid to say that it is not the piece of paper that constitutes a genuine marriage.

Imagine, if you will, that you and your steady are the sole survivors of a horrible shipwreck. You wash up on a deserted island and you are absolutely alone. Suppose you both decide that since this is where you may spend the rest of your lives, and since you love each other, you want to become husband and wife. What should you do? Would the wise and Christian thing be to divide the island in half so each of you can stay on his own side as you fight temptation? Should you go ahead and have sex and then ask God for His forgiveness each morning for what took place the night before?

Or would it be decent, proper, and even godly to simply tell God of your intentions to live in a permanent relationship as husband and wife and then get on with the honeymoon? This, in fact, is what isolated Early American pioneers often did since it might be two or three years before a pastor made his circuit to officially solemnize the marriage. Why would people of strict Puritan background do this? Because at the very core of what it means to be married is the promise of lifelong responsibility and commitment to the other person. If the two people getting married are Christians, that promise of commitment is made not only to each other, but also to God. Because the couple on the island or the pioneers had no choice but to officiate their own wedding, and because the essential ingredient is the promise given to each other and to God, they would be just as solemnly married as any couple who marched down the aisle of a huge church.

This does not mean that living together without marriage is okay if you have the understanding that you will be committed for life. For example, just because two people made promises to be committed to each other on a passionate, star-studded night does not mean that they are married. Genuine marriage involves a great deal more responsibility and action than hot-blooded intent. But we must recognize that what people say about the "piece of paper" not being the validation of marriage has a ring of truth to it.

In reality, those who humbug the "piece of paper" but who are truly committed for life to one person are just playing a word game. They act, live, speak, and carry the same responsibility as those who are married legally. There is no real difference except for the public and legal formalities. On the other hand, those who use this line of reasoning dishonestly, who talk commitment but are really looking for an easy way to satisfy their lust, are among the scumballs of the earth. They are Indian givers in the disguise of honest people. In their determination to satisfy their needs they leave a trail of broken hearts.

Marriage is a universal social custom. For Christians in particular it is not only social but also spiritual. The ritual followed in order to become married is not the issue. It would be very brash to suggest that people in some jungle tribe are any less married because they smeared the blood of a dead monkey on the forehead of their bride as a sign of their commitment rather than signing a marriage certificate. Again, it is the vow that makes the marriage, not the legal technicalities.

C.S. Lewis held strongly to the idea that Christian marriages were of a different kind than were the state contracts of non-Christians. He went so far in this thinking that late in his life he married an American woman in a strictly civil (secular) ceremony. He did this because she was a good friend and he wanted to help her. His friend wanted to continue to live in England, but had stayed as long as was legally permitted. Marrying Lewis, who was a Briton, fulfilled a legal requirement so that this woman and her two small children could stay.

Lewis saw his marriage as a mere legal contract motivated by compassion. He had papers drawn up that made clear his position. To him, he was still just as much a confirmed bachelor as ever. He had no intention of consummating the marriage. The "couple" lived apart in their own homes and maintained social contact. While this kind of situation is called marriage by the state, it obviously is not anything close to what we understand marriage to be.

Interestingly, C.S. Lewis eventually fell in love with his legal wife and genuinely married her in a Christian ceremony. They had a blissful and joyous marriage that was cut short by his wife's death from cancer.

All this may lead you to ask, "If a marriage is not the

piece of paper, why bother with it?"

Of course the reverse can also be asked, "If you are really committed to each other for life why not prove it to the world by a public, legal marriage?"

Christians become legally married for several reasons. One is that we are taught to obey the law of the land in which we live. Another is that by having a wedding, marriage certificate and all, we are proudly declaring our intent and commitment to the community at large, to our friends, to our family, and to our spouse. Going back to our couple who were washed up on a deserted island, it would follow that when they are rescued, they should go through with public and legal recognition of their private vows.

Another consideration in the legal aspects of marriage is that it gives legitimacy to any children who might be born to the couple. This has been, historically, one of the most important reasons for legal marriage.

Ironically, those who wish to escape the complications that come with marriage by simply living together for the rest of their lives will find that most states view any cohabitation for at least seven years as a "common law" marriage. In other words, if one party was to bail out on the other, the court would treat the couple like any other couple getting a divorce.

Usually, at best, the people who say that they are permanently committed to their partner for life, but want to avoid the paperwork, are a bit immature. They want to sound like they are living dangerously when they are really living just like any other married couple on the block.

Reason 2
We need to see if we are compatible.

On the surface this sounds sensible. As proponents of

this life-style explain, "Would you buy a pair of shoes without trying them on?" "Well," they continue, "why marry someone with whom you are not compatible?"

Why indeed? In fact, why live with them at all? Could it be that these relationships are built on the physical level far more than they are built on knowing the person who resides in the body? For many this kind of rationale is a clever way of saying, "I'm too horny to wait to find out if I really like this person." But it sounds much more acceptable to say, "We need to see if we are compatible."

For others this reasoning means "I'll live with this person as long as we get along, but once I don't get my way, I'm outta here!" These poor simpletons sooner or later will have to face the fact that there will be no one with whom they will never have a conflict.

What sets marriage apart and makes it desirable above all other situations is the idea that two people are committed to each other to work out their difficulties, not to run away from them. For most people, compatibility in marriage is something that comes from two people working the puzzle pieces of their personalities around so that they interlock with each other.

Sometimes people may be compatible initially, but because of various traumas or difficulties they may become tough to live with at some point later in life. Does this mean that they are to be abandoned?

The kind of relationship living together creates is full of conditions. The people in this kind of relationship cannot help but feel the pressure and the tentativeness of it. They cannot let down their guards and really be themselves without the danger of being discarded like a shoe that doesn't fit just right.

Finding someone with whom you are compatible is a good thing. But it does not take living together to figure out compatibility. To use the analogy of the shoe again, the main thing is to be sure you have found a shoe that is the right size, you will always have to wear it for a while for it to become comfortable to you. And store managers won't let you do that unless you buy it!

Closely related to the compatibility cop-out is the idea that people should only be together as long as they love each other. Once the love dies away, they are free to fly to some other love interest. This is often expressed, "We don't know if it will work out."

Once again the couple involved with this line of reasoning is cautious and guarded. They know that they cannot fully rely on the other person to be there at all times. This deep sense of being unsettled infects every part of the relationship.

Another common reason for living together is:

Reason 3
*I've been burned once and I'm not going to
get burned again.*

Often the people who say this are those who were once married, but who have experienced a bitter divorce and the collapse of all their expectations. Sometimes they are people who come from homes where they suffered through the divorce of parents. Whatever the background, they are people who are afraid to trust completely, to put themselves out on the firing line of commitment. They will not surrender their lives to anyone again.

Most of these people are tragic figures whose lives are caving in on them. They refuse to give of themselves or to trust with their whole hearts. They never allow themselves to be vulnerable to the sting of another and by lacking that vulnerability, they live an unbalanced and incomplete life.

This attitude spills over into their live-in relationship. They give enough to keep their partner around at least for a while. But once real transparency and trust is called for, they retreat. The relationship can go nowhere. It is shallow, usually based only on physical gratification.

Reason 4
We are going to get married one of these days.

This is a very popular reason for living together today. The obvious questions that this line brings to mind is "What's stopping you?" Usually the response is that there are plans to make, finances to take care of, and/or school to finish. All the while the couple is living very much like they would if they were married anyway.

Often in these cases there is one party who very much wants the commitment of marriage and has managed to squeeze out of the other party a vague promise to get married "one of these days." Both parties in the relationship try to be content, the one having at least a glimmer of hope for a long-term relationship and the other being able to stall things off for a while.

Reason 5
I'm lonely.

Being lonely is often a reason people give for living together. Just having another person around can fill the void and make loneliness more bearable for a while. This is particularly true for people who find themselves divorced and alone after years of marriage.

Often these people are more pathetic than evil. They

just want to be loved, but they will settle for being used. It is not too uncommon to find people who fit this pattern using each other until their emotions are in better health.

Tragically these people fail to lean upon the very One who will not only support them, but will revitalize them as well.

Reason 6
I've already gone too far. I might as well go all the way.

This rationale is commonly given by Christians who have failed to keep themselves sexually pure. They figure that since they have fallen into the sin of pre-marital sex already, they have nothing left to lose by living together. Naturally, what persons in this condition need to confront are the biblical principles that will help them seek the forgiveness they need and the strength to get out and stay out of a wrong situation. Often the real problem with persons who give this reason for living with another is that they really don't want to be led from their sin.

Reason 7
If it doesn't work out, it is better to have just lived with someone than it is to have the stain of divorce.

Like many of the excuses we have already evaluated, there is some truth to the preceding statement. Monitor your feelings as you read the following: someone you know has been divorced five times; someone else you know has lived with five different partners. If you are like most people, you would think of the divorced person as a flake and of the other person as perhaps a little mixed up. People do take divorce more seriously for the simple reason that marriage means promises and commitment. Having several divorces is an indication that the person involved has some serious personality flaw or that he is a poor judge of character.

The Bottom Line

The primary danger of living together comes from what it lacks: genuine commitment. Every couple who involves themselves in this kind of relationship sooner or later comes face-to-face with the instability that is the trademark of their living arrangement. At any time one party or the other can simply "take his or her cookies and go home." There are no legal binds, nothing that is "ours." The party who decides to go simply gathers together his belongings and moves out. Of course this same thing can and is done in a marriage situation, but not without far more complications. But even if the legal requirements for parting are simple with the couple who has been living together, the degree of pain felt by separation can be just as great.

Lack of commitment infects relationships in subtle ways. For example, one recent study indicated that people who were married had a more fulfilling sexual relationship than did those who were living together. The researchers' conclusion was that the lack of commitment on the part of the people who were living together spilled over even into their sex lives so that they could not give sex their all. Married couples who had made a lifetime commitment had more satisfaction in their sex lives.

Relationships of those who are living together are far more embedded with fatal faults than are the relationships of those who are married. For this reason, the odds of living together forever are even less favorable than are the odds of remaining married to the same person forever (about a 50/50 chance). Of course, some people do not want their relationships to succeed. Some selfish people are more intrigued by the idea of a succession of lovers and roommates who can simply be discarded when they become boring.

Living together also says something about the inner lives of the persons involved. Living together can be the ultimate in self-centeredness. It reflects an attitude of wanting all of the joy and benefits of marriage, but without the responsibility or risks that a permanent relationship brings. The reason most people really don't want to get married is because they want a convenient escape hatch to disappear into if things get tough. They think in the terms of "me" and "mine" rather than "we" and "ours." They are Indian givers with their love. They hold the right to reclaim it at any time by virtue of their lack of promises.

Finally, people who call themselves Christians while living with others out of wedlock are seriously damaging their witness to non-Christians. Their life-style is in conflict with God's commandments. God did not mention exceptions when He commanded that we get rid of, or put to death, whatever belongs to our earthly nature. And, He topped the list of sins with sexual immorality (see Col. 3:5). To live against God's will is to hold up to ridicule the very claim of being a Christian.

Sadly, many who are living together have a very poor idea of what genuine love is all about. They know (or care) little about commitment. They often end up ripping off their partner emotionally, physically, and spiritually. And they rob themselves of the kind of relationship that God declares is best for us: the kind of relationship in which we will grow and will be fulfilled.

4

Women and the Church: Shared Leadership or Male Headship?

Annette Parrish

Outside a cold, gray rain steadily pelted the windows. But inside the church sanctuary it seemed warm. Fourteen-year-old Amy closed her eyes as she listened to the words of the worship choruses. It was the first Sunday of the month and in this medium-sized California church, that meant communion would be shared in the morning service.

Communion Sunday always affected Amy positively.

She felt the comfort that comes from being a part of a body of believers. She was awed by participating in a symbolic meal that had been shared in unbroken history by millions of believers since Jesus first shared it with His disciples.

As the pastor asked the twelve elders to come forward to distribute the bread, Amy opened her eyes. For the first time something invaded upon her peaceful reflections. Amy felt as though she had been struck across her face. Her cheeks flushed with resentment, she turned to her mother and said, "Why are the elders all men?"

Meanwhile in a different building in the same town another group of Christians gathered to worship. Stepping to the pulpit, Bible in hand, the pastor looked out at the congregation. The church had grown. Esther opened the Bible and began her sermon.

Halfway across the United States a visiting woman missionary from the Philippines was startled when several churches would not allow her to share the pulpit with her husband. She was told by the senior pastor at one of these churches that his flock strictly follows the biblical instruction "Women should be silent in church" (see 1 Cor. 14:34). Having been raised in China where her mother preached to Chinese congregations and having served in the Philippines where she often took the pulpit, Kari was very perplexed. She was even further bewildered when she attended some women's Bible studies where color analysis (figuring out which clothing colors are the most flattering), cooking, and the home arts seemed to be more important than the great truths of the Bible.

The issue of how women should serve was also confronting Pastor Norris. He had just come out of one of the most disturbing church board meetings of his long career. It all had to do with hiring an associate pastor. A very capable woman had applied for the job and although in his denomination the local church was empowered to ordain and hire women, his congregation was split on whether it would be right. In the board meeting sincere Christians with solid Bible backgrounds had hotly debated scriptural teaching regarding women in the Church. To make matters worse, this group of believers seemed to be focusing on the controversy instead of on their unity in Christ and how they should be serving Him in the community. But who was right? Pastor Norris retired to his office to spend long hours praying and studying Scriptures relating to the issue.

The controversy surrounding how women should serve the Church can be confusing. Bible scholars differ on how key verses dealing with women should be interpreted. Cultural standards and church tradition seem to further complicate the issue. Some see women pushing for more involvement in the Church to be a result of the feminist movement. Others see the effort to keep women out of certain positions as a backlash against the same movement. But this issue did not originate in the twentieth century. In fact, its roots go back many, many centuries.

Some History

Although the Old Testament records that Israel had women rulers (Deborah, Athaliah) and women prophets (Miriam, Deborah, Huldah), the culture in which Jesus ministered in the first century was one that openly discriminated against women. Many Pharisees started their day with a prayer that went something like this: "I thank God that I was not born a slave, a Gentile, or a woman."

Ancestry was recorded through the fathers (check out

the "begets" in the Bible). Crowds were counted according to how many men were present; women and children were not taken into account (see John 6:10).

Jesus demonstrated a radical departure from the culture of His day. He praised the faith of women. He allowed Mary, the sister of Martha, to sit at His feet, a place of honor, while He taught. Jesus seemed to assume that women were capable not only of learning and understanding but also of engaging in debate.[1] Many women, including Mary Magdalene, Joanna, and Susanna, traveled with Jesus and His disciples, supporting them with their own funds and listening while Jesus preached.

After Jesus returned to heaven, women retained their improved position for a while. Although the structure of society had not changed, attitudes within the body of believers had.

Women attended early church gatherings with their husbands and children. They prophesied in these meetings. They participated in communion. And, they suffered martyrdom along with their Christian brothers.

Women were also allowed certain roles in the leadership of the Church in the first and second centuries. It is likely that women, such as Phoebe, held the position of deacon (see Rom. 16:1,2)[2]. There is a difference of opinion in church circles as to whether women were excluded from the offices of elder and pastor. The majority of church groups believe women did not hold these offices. However some believe that under certain conditions they did. They cite the example of a woman named Junias (see Rom. 16:7) who may have been an apostle (a highly controversial position) and historical evidence such as the discovery of a wall painting in the catacombs of Rome that pictures seven women distributing communion, a duty performed by pastors and elders.

Bible scholars also differ as to whether the instruction "I do not permit a woman to teach" (1 Tim. 2:12) was directed by the apostle Paul to certain churches or to all churches and for all time. Some interpret this instruction as meaning women can teach children and other women, but not men. But it is evident that one woman, a close friend of the apostle Paul named Priscilla, taught an important man in the early church, Apollos. It may be important to note that Priscilla taught Apollos in her home, not at a church gathering.

Slowly, as the years passed, women began to lose ground. As the Church grew, their meetings became more formal. Gatherings that had been characterized by sharing, prayer, singing of hymns, and prophesying began to follow certain forms called liturgies. Men who served as pastors, and who had always taught and shepherded groups of Christians became recognized as *the* leaders of specific congregations. Pastors began to lead the church services, reading from the Scriptures and teaching what the Scriptures meant. Prophesying, an activity in which women had been allowed to participate, became uncommon.[3]

Congregations were organized into larger groups headed by men called bishops. As the hierarchal system grew, more offices were added: archbishop, cardinal, pope. Women did not serve in these offices.

However, with the changing church structure, certain new positions did open to women. Around the fourth century, retreats, which we now call convents, opened. Women who renounced the normal life of marrying and caring for a family could go to these retreats and dedicate their lives to prayer and charitable works. At around the same time, similar retreats which would come to be known as monasteries opened for men.

Women and men from these retreats communicated and joined together in projects to further God's Kingdom. Notably, Jerome, who first translated the Bible into a language that the average person of the day could understand (the Vulgate), said that he profited in his work from the criticism and questioning of Marcella, a Christian woman who understood Greek and Hebrew and whose home had become a center for prayer and study.

Events in history gave the monasteries and convents another important role. As the years rolled by, Rome lost power. Barbarian hordes invaded cities, ravaging and burning. Much of the literature of the early Church and many of the oldest copies of Scriptures survived the pillage because the works were hidden by dedicated Christians in convents and monasteries.

By the fifth century, tribes of barbarians were invading Rome itself. Often Christian women were carried off as hostages or captives. Much of the evangelization of Northern Europe was done by these women witnessing to their captor husbands.

But as women lost ground socially throughout the Dark Ages and the Middle Ages, they also lost position and respect in the Church. When as a result of the Reformation, monasteries and convents were abolished in Protestant denominations, women no longer had an office in which they could serve. They entered into a period of powerlessness and dishonor that would last for many years. The situation was so bad that an English pastor, John Donne, raised quite a controversy by proposing that it might be possible in rare instances that a few women could have a few virtues. It is even more outrageous that another of Donne's proposals was considered controversial in the 1600s: Donne believed that women possessed souls.

Into this atmosphere of repression came a glimmer of hope. The Bible was being translated into languages that common people understood. This had not been done since the fourth century when Jerome translated it into the Vulgate.

In 1611 the King James Bible became available to English-speaking people. Christians who hungered to read God's Word began earnest Bible study. One of these Christians was George Fox, the founder of the Quakers. The Bible led Fox to new understanding of what it means to be a Christian. Along with other unwelcome ideas, Fox's group of Christians believed in the "priesthood of all believers." Women were allowed to speak in church meetings. But this innovation was not well received. George Fox and many of his followers were often imprisoned or whipped. Some Quakers were executed both in England and in the United States.

In the 1700s a great revival which would influence women's role in the Church began in England and the United States. John Wesley, founder of the Methodist Church, was one of the leaders of this movement that encouraged Bible reading, prayer, and repentance of sins. Wesley appointed women as itinerant preachers, at first limiting them to five minute talks, then gradually increasing the time they were allowed to speak. This trend of allowing women to speak in church continued with the Holiness Movement of the 1800s. Outstanding among women preachers in the 1800s was Catherine Booth, co-founder of the Salvation Army.

Also in the 1800s, Christian women united with other women in two great political movements: one, to abolish slavery, and the other, to gain the right of women to vote. Both of these movements got strong support from some Christians and bitter opposition from others.

The brakes began to be applied to women's increased involvement in the Church in the 1920s. Churches of the Methodist and Holiness Movements had become very well established in society. They became more structured and with this structure came the desire of the church members to be led not by itinerate preachers, but by pastors who had attended seminary. Since most families sent only their sons to institutes of higher learning, and since most seminaries did not admit women, pulpits began to close to women.[4]

Status Report

Today different denominations or congregations take different positions on how women should serve the Church. These positions fall into three basic patterns.

Those who maintain that men alone were ordained by God to govern the Church hold to the view of *hierarchism*. These Christians base their view on New Testament Scriptures (1 Cor. 11:3; 12:12,13; 14:26-40; 1 Tim. 2:11-14) and on something called the creation ordinance.[5] The creation ordinance has four basic arguments taken from Genesis 2 which are used to show the subordination of women to men:

1. Woman was created after the man and is therefore secondary to him.
2. Woman was "taken from the man" and therefore secondary to him.
3. Woman was named by man and is therefore subordinate to him.
4. Woman was created to be a "helper" for man and as such is subordinate to him.

But in recent years many evangelical scholars have rejected all or part of the hierarchal position. Some of these Christians take the position that Scripture is better interpreted by a model that stresses partnership between men and women. They do not see the Genesis account as ordaining women to be forever subordinate to men.

Christians who hold this *egalitarian* position usually believe that when God said to Eve, "Your desire will be for your husband and he will rule over you" (Gen. 3:16), He was predicting a result of the Fall and was not setting in motion a model He ordained. They answer the four arguments of the creation ordinance with explanations similar to these:

1. Being created first does not imply superiority since frogs, cows, and fish were all created before Adam.
2. Eve being taken from Adam stresses their unity/relatedness.[6]
3. In the original language, the word translated "called" (Gen. 2:23) does not imply authority. It is different from the Hebrew word for "named" or "called" that is used when Adam named the animals. The word used in conjunction with Adam naming Eve does not imply Adam's authority.
4. The word translated as "helper" (Gen. 2:18) is used nineteen times in the Old Testament. Fifteen times it is used to describe God. So the word "helper" itself cannot imply inferiority or subordination.[7]

Many of the Christians who believe that the model for

the Church is shared leadership believe that the apostle Paul's instructions for women to be silent in church were directed at specific situations in a few churches of the first century. They point out that historical tradition did not totally exclude women since Israel had had women rulers (Deborah, Athaliah) and women prophets (Miriam, Deborah, Huldah, Anna). These Christians feel that the overriding principle of equality in Christ (see Gal. 3:26-29) deserves more stress than patterns of church structure which can be interpreted from the original Greek to mean different things.

A growing number of Christians' viewpoints fall somewhere between the hierarchal and egalitarian models. Most mainstream Protestant churches would fit in this third category. Although 80 percent of these churches do not prohibit the ordination of women, they overwhelmingly, by denominational policy or simply by practice, are led by male senior pastors. Women are increasingly visible in other positions.

Christians in this middle ground stress that there are many different opportunities for serving in the Body and that these functions are equal in honor (see Rom. 12:5, 1 Cor. 12:5,6). In positions of authority women are most likely to be found as directors of Christian education, on mission boards, or teaching Sunday School. They may serve as deacons. Less frequently they are seen in the roles of elder or pastor.

What Should We Do?

Every Christian should consider the issue of how women should serve the Church. (That women should serve in some capacity is not in question.) A primary concern in looking into this issue must be sound biblical interpretation. Two basic questions need to be asked of every passage studied:

1. What was God saying through His human servant to the first hearers or readers of the message?
2. How should we understand and apply the passage to people today?

To answer the second of these questions, readers must understand that most of the teaching and commands in the Bible fall into one of two categories:

1. unchanging highest ideals, norms, or standards, or
2. regulations for people where they were.

Keeping in mind these guidelines, there are several important questions that need to be examined in light of Scripture:

- Should women be allowed to preach and teach in church? What limitations, if any, should be applied to their preaching and teaching?
- What offices should be open to women? What is the scriptural basis for this position?
- How has society affected Christians' views on this topic?
- What should be the motivation for leadership?

While the issue of *how* women should serve is very important, it is more important that all Christians *continue to serve their Lord with a spirit of joy*. It is the Christian's privilege to know that God is perfectly just and loving in

His dealings with His people. This includes how He desires each Christian, male or female, to serve Him. As His instruments on earth, we must reflect Him by submitting to His will and to each other. In doing this we can better demonstrate His love to each other and to a hurting world.

Notes

1. Mary Evans, *Women in the Bible* (Downers Grove: InterVarsity Press, 1983), p. 51.
2. Alvera and Berkeley Mickelsen, "What Happens to God's Gifts?" *The Standard*, May 1984, p. 37.
3. Kari Torjesen Malcolm, *Women at the Crossroads* (Downers Grove: InterVarsity Press, 1982), p. 93-95.
4. Ibid., pp. 119-133.
5. John Piper, "How Should a Woman Lead?" *The Standard*, May 1984, p. 34.
6. Francis A. Schaeffer, *Genesis in Space & Time* (Downers Grove: InterVarsity Press, 1972), pp. 46,47.
7. Evans, *Women in the Bible*, p. 16.

Some Scriptures to Study

Luke 10:38-42—In this passage, Jesus affirmed that women should put Him first, before all other concerns.

Romans 16:1-3,6,7,12—These verses mention women who served the early Church.

1 Corinthians 11:3-16—Women are instructed to cover their heads in worship services. Some interpreters feel that this is a sign of submission that is still valid. Others say that it is a sign of a woman's own authority and relationship with God.

1 Corinthians 12:12,13—All Christians are equal in Christ and have a unique role in His Body.

1 Corinthians 14:26-40 and 1 Timothy 2:11-15—These passages are usually interpreted one of two ways: (1) Women should not preach or teach in public services or (2) This verse was a specific instruction to a particular situation where women were being disruptive.

Galatians 3:26-29—Another passage that stresses the believers' unity in Christ.

Ephesians 5:21-33—This passage describes God's plan for Christian marriage. Although both husbands and wives are told to submit to each other, the husband is in the position of authority.

1 Timothy 3:1-13—This passage describes the qualifications required of elders and deacons.

5

Interracial Dating and Marriage: Is It Biblical?

Jon Trott

We were at the Great America amusement park with our kids, just having a good time. All of a sudden it seemed like everyone we passed was staring at us and whispering. All these suburban white families were gawking at my husband's black skin and at our kids and me like we were from another planet. I wanted to go home.

Western civilization has a dark, sometimes violent past when it comes to racism. In the United States blacks have been enslaved, Indians have been massacred, and Chinese workers have been picked out to be the victims of robbery and murder. During World War II Japanese Americans were put in detention camps. Similar examples could be cited for many other "civilized" western nations.

But many if not most people think that racism is a thing of the past. As one recent movie character put it, "Racism? This is the Cosby decade!"

Most racists won't stand out in a crowd. They can be very polite, kind people. Few would call a black person that word that is a profane twist on the word Negro. All would smile at a Hispanic baby. But where the "rubber meets the road" for the average person who considers himself or herself free from bigotry is in the area of inter-racial dating and marriage.

Often, friendship is more rewarding and less risky than the dating game. Friendships are where communication across racial lines should and usually does begin. But what if things move from friendship to romantic interest?

> I kind of liked this one black guy and we were just getting to know each other. I was 14. I think he was 15. When my mother found out that he was asking about me after summer camp, she must have let him know that she didn't approve. I don't know what she said to him, but he never came around any more.

What is racism? Webster's dictionary defines it as "a belief that race is the primary determinant of human traits and capacities and that racial differences produce an inherent superiority of a particular race." Whew. Not too appealing.

Think about someone you know who's addicted to

alcohol or drugs. It's hard to understand the addicted person's actions unless you're addicted yourself, isn't it? But what about getting drunk once in a while? Or smoking a little pot? If the situation is right, even a Christian can fall for this sort of temptation.

The same thing can happen with racism. People like those in the Ku Klux Klan and other extremist groups are the junkies of racism. But normal closet racists don't run around in sheets any more than the occasional drunk goes around exhibiting his or her weakness. The closet racist may even be unaware of the subtle control prejudice has over his or her thoughts and actions.

All the gentle reasoning or angry shouting in the world won't bring racists around. In short, racism is a heart condition, not a head condition. And only Jesus can change a heart.

Racism and Scripture Twisting

How should a Christian view interracial dating and marriage? On any question of importance the Scriptures themselves should be the focus of our search for an answer. What does God's Word have to say about marriage and romantic relationships in general? And, even if Scripture gives interracial relationships the okay, what about the pressures society will put on them? Is it selfish or foolish to enter into such a relationship?

A few of the classic arguments against so-called *miscegenation* (a fancy, negative word to describe a marriage between two persons of different races) are Bible-based—supposedly. Keep in mind the culture that invented many of these theories was one that had to come up with "moral" reasons to support slavery.

An important passage segregationists use from Scripture is the story of Noah cursing Ham's son, Canaan. Ham saw Noah lying drunk and naked in his tent. He went to his brothers and told them what he had seen. Instead of embarrassing their father further the brothers put a garment over their shoulders and backed into Noah's tent, covering him without looking at him. For Ham's shameful behavior, Noah directed this curse against Ham's son: "The lowest of slaves will he be to his brothers" (Gen. 9:25). The punch line? Ham's children, according to racist tradition, were black.

How much validity is there to this interpretation of the story of Noah's sons? None. The flaw is that the descendants of Canaan were the Canaanites, a Caucasian (white) people. So much for the view that blacks are under a curse and those who oppress them are only fulfilling Scripture.

Another racist twisting of Scripture centers on Cain. According to avid segregationists, God marked Cain by giving him black skin after Cain killed his brother Abel. This well-known argument is still used, despite the overwhelming rejection of it by Bible scholars. For although God did mark Cain in some way, the Bible doesn't even hint that this mark was black skin.

We can learn one valuable lesson from these examples of Scripture twisting: a reader can put things into a Bible verse or passage that aren't there in reality. In order not to fall prey to these twisted interpretations, each Christian should examine the Scriptures for himself.

Mongrelizing the Races?

The real point being made by all of these segregationists' arguments is that there is a need to preserve "racial purity." Finis Jennings Dake, a leading speaker for the segregationists, found a way to reinterpret Genesis to support the idea that by mixing races we're contaminating God's creation. Says Dake: God "made everything to produce 'after his own kind' . . . kind means type and color or He would have kept them all alike to begin with."

How far can the Scripture be twisted? The word "type" is meant to apply to species of animals and makes no sense if used to apply to human beings. (See Gen. 1:24.) All people are the same type except for minute differences of skin, eye, and hair color, or differences of height and weight, personality traits and talents. If one couple, namely, Adam and Eve, are the genetic parents of all people, how can anyone say people come in different types? Do skin pigments or facial characteristics matter to God? Furthermore, if God really wanted us to keep our skin colors pure, why not our hair and eye colors as well? Should blondes only marry blondes?

Another example of the "big twist": a common objection to intermingling of the races, or as ultra-fundamentalist Bob Jones, Jr., called it "the mongrelization of the races," concerns God's Old Testament warning to Israel not to intermarry with the surrounding peoples. Many have claimed this refers to interracial marriages: "Miscegenation caused Israel to be judged by God." In this we see racial bias blinding people to the clear meaning of Scripture. Two separate issues, spiritual purity and racial purity, are confused here. God is concerned *only* with the intermarrying of believers with unbelievers. God's people marrying worshipers of false idols led to judgment, because when men of Israel married unbelievers, they usually began following the idolatrous practices of their wives.

The most bizarre theory offered by racists is the idea that blacks are the offspring of demons. This groundless theory isn't worth further time. I mention it only as an extreme example of how far the Scriptures can be bent by those searching to justify their crooked beliefs.

"These people that say blacks don't have souls, that we can't go to heaven, well, that's something I won't even discuss," says John, a 36-year-old black married to a white woman. John, a believer for 12 years, anguished, "How far can these people go? Do they have the tiniest idea of how they make me feel?"

It is the racist who falls under God's judgment. He will be judged because of his idols: gods of skin color or other outward physical or cultural features. As black evangelical John Perkins says, "Racism is the raising up of a false idol—race—against the True God of Scripture." This is in direct opposition to the teaching of the Bible. "Man looks at the outward appearance," said God to Samuel, "but the Lord looks at the heart" (1 Sam. 16:7). All who accept Christ's Lordship are part of His chosen people. "There is neither Jew nor Greek, slave nor free, male nor female, for you are all one in Christ Jesus. If you belong to Christ, then you are Abraham's seed, and heirs according to the promise" (Gal. 3:28,29).

Those who oppose interracial marriage have based their argument on an erroneous presupposition: race matters to God. We can boldly state that it does not because of the evidence given us by Scripture. It is no accident that the Body of believers, the Church, is described as a human body, which cannot be divided (segregated) without harm to itself. No human being is less able to receive the Holy Spirit than any other: "We are all baptized by one Spirit into one body—whether Jews or Greeks, slave or free—and we were all given the one Spirit to drink" (1 Cor. 12:13). That Spirit erases, or to put it more accurately, transcends, the cultural/ethnic/racial differences between people.

This applies to the final, and false, argument used by racists: black, brown, white, yellow, and red Christians can still be equal although separate. History shows us that where such a doctrine has existed, its practice has always led to the oppression of one or more races while lifting up another. Our most blatant modern-day example of this is South Africa's apartheid system.

Being a respecter of persons is condemned powerfully by James: "If you really keep the royal law found in Scripture, 'Love your neighbor as yourself,' you are doing right. But if you show favoritism, you sin and are convicted by the law as lawbreakers" (Jas. 2:8,9). For a revealing study on Scripture's attitude toward discrimination in general, read the entire second chapter of James.

The Ones You Love Won't Like It

There are no biblical objections to two believers of different races marrying. But that doesn't mean that interracial relationships are easy. In all my discussions with interracial couples, I found that the number one objectors to the couples' marriages were their own families.

Lyda, a soft-spoken white woman married to Ron, an equally soft-spoken black man, notes, "I think the main bigotry that we find is through our family. I have an aunt and uncle who have not spoken to me since my husband and I started dating. They even wrote a nasty letter when we announced our engagement. I think my family has been the main point of pressure we've experienced."

"Though it was no problem for us, it was for our parents," said Barb, a black woman married to Eric, a white. "It was a question of how our children would be raised, what their racial identity would be, and what kind of persecution and pressure they would face." Barb paused to comfort her crying newborn daughter. "What we found out is this: interracial couples make beautiful children.

"Our marriage has been used by God to help both our families," Barb continued. "Eric's family never knew any blacks before me. My family has gotten an education too. My mom always disliked whites, but now Eric is around. He's not just 'a white man.' He's my husband, Eric. And that really has worked on my mother's attitudes. She wouldn't speak to me when we first got engaged. But then Eric's mom, who's a Christian and was also struggling over our engagement, got together with my mom. And that really got my mother thinking!"

Obviously, there are some points an interracial couple considering marriage should ponder carefully. Is the couple ready for the stares of passersby, some friendly, some not? Are they ready for that certain cool aloofness suburban-bred northern whites can turn on when disapproving? And are they ready for incidents like the one which occurred to one of my best friends, a white minister, and his wife, who happens to be black?

Could You Take the Abuse?

Jason and Joanne (not their real names) were invited to a Christian friend's wedding in a Chicago suburb. But at the reception things turned anything but joyful for this couple. First, when Joanne, a black woman, approached the bride's mother, she was pointedly ignored. "I couldn't believe how rude she was."

Many empty chairs lined the various tables, but when Joanne's white husband, Jason, tried to seat his wife and himself, someone would inform them that the seats were taken. This happened once too often for Joanne. "Jason wasn't picking up on the stares we were getting. But I think as a black person I'm more experienced in sensing bigotry."

Jason, to test Joanne's assertion, went to a table alone and asked if two places were empty; the reply was yes. When he brought Joanne to the table, however, a stunned silence enveloped the table. Then, quickly the entire table of whites got up and left.

"There we sat, alone at this table . . . I just wanted to get up and leave," said Joanne.

The two sat alone until a group of hard-drinking people in the corner of the room asked them over. "We saw how those Christians are treating you," said one. "Come and sit with us black sheep over in the corner."

"Usually I'm not upset when people act like that," says Joanne, "because they're unsaved, so what can you expect? But when Christians act that way . . . well, I have a hard time thinking of them as Christians. I guess it's like any other area a person doesn't turn over to the Lord; you can be that way and still be a Christian, but before the Lord it's unacceptable behavior."

And it isn't just white people who practice prejudice. Another interracial couple suffered at the hands of the wife's brothers, who felt that her "black purity" was being contaminated by her white husband. Before the marriage, one brother even threatened to kill his sister. "Your kids will have white blood. Don't you have any pride in your race?" She reflected, "There's a difference between black pride and black bigotry."

And in the splitting of cultural hairs department, a Puerto Rican friend related to me his first experience with his wife's mother, a Guatemalan. "I wanted my daughter to marry someone from her own country, certainly not a Puerto Rican," she said to him bluntly. Though he could laugh about it in retrospect, he admitted, "I was really hurt by that. Funny, though, there are whites who look at both my wife and me as 'those latinos.'"

Henry, a Chinese Christian married to a white, believes his own race's problems here are more subtle. "For Chinese born in this country (the United States), the worst problem is our rejection of our own racial and cultural background. My generation wanted to be American, and that meant tossing out our own heritage. I refused, for instance, to date Oriental women, because that was identifying with Chinese culture. I was accepted by my white friends, but Orientals concerned with holding on to aspects of our culture were angry with me. Fortunately, because Christianity freed me from having to 'conform' to Western culture, I have learned to treasure my parents' heritage as well as this country's. When I felt the Lord leading me to marry Julie, a white woman, I didn't have to be introspective about betraying my heritage because I'd accepted the fact that my culture was a God-created part of me."

Where Does Jesus Christ Fit In?

The interracial couples I spoke to all said that their faith in Jesus Christ is absolutely the only basis for their marriage. "If I'd been a non-Christian I'd have left John for sure," says Mary. "I was afraid of being an outcast, of people thinking I wasn't okay. I was afraid of him being black, because there was a lot in me that didn't want that stigma put on me. But once I became a Christian I understood life from a whole different perspective; I understood what life was really about. I wasn't afraid any more. I didn't have to worry about what other people thought, because it really didn't matter. What I was concerned about now was following Jesus."

All the couples I interviewed, especially black/white couples, emphasized the limitations of where they could live. "You want to find a place that's a mixture," says Erle, a black man of 39 years. "You don't want to live in an all-black area or an all-white area. Around colleges is good. When we lived in Chicago, Rogers Park was a place like that."

The couples I spoke with also said that the Church is their most important marriage support. Barb and Eric live in a full-time Christian community called Jesus People U.S.A. "Living in a full-time Christian fellowship," says Eric, "the racial issue becomes less important than it would if we were attending an average church, and far less important than if we weren't Christians. The whole issue of dating and marriage across racial lines is volatile—HOT!—when you do it in our still segregated society. In our community, race is a non-issue."

John and Mary were members of an otherwise all-black Christian community, and for Mary, the non-judgmental acceptance she found from her brothers and sisters in the Lord was foundational: "Black people are more ready to accept an interracial marriage than white people. Even now, I have black women come up to me and tell me how beautiful my children are. I have never had a white woman—other than a friend—do that. I'm not trying to say blacks are better than whites, but because they've felt the pain of being oppressed and rejected themselves, I think they often are more aware of other people's needs for support.

"By living with black people, my husband and the other Christians of the community we were in, I learned things that most whites don't know. People are the same—goods and bads included!"

What sort of lessons can interracial couples teach us? John says, "I feel like I have a mission to open people's minds, to say, 'Hey listen, we're just two people. Nothing more, nothing less. We're capable of feeling love and hurt and all the other things. In the fallen world we live in, a couple like us is going to be hurt and judged, but God brought us together; He'll preserve and strengthen our marriage despite the world's opinion.'"

Putting First Things First

How can a couple from different racial backgrounds know they are called to serve God together? Scripture commands believers not to be unequally yoked with unbelievers, and to ignore this command is to create a relationship or marriage that is full of pain and conflict. The bottom line then is to make sure both partners have the same desire to serve God. Pray together, get counsel from trusted older Christians. The foundational goals and aspirations of the Christian husband and wife, to serve God and to walk in His will, should be the same no matter what racial or cultural backgrounds are involved.

An interracial couple will experience a full spectrum of joys and frustrations. And, like any other couple, in times of stress they may go for the low blow, saying hurtful things. In these cases bigotry may raise its ugly head. Every husband, angry with his wife, has had at least the fleeting thought, "Maybe this was a mistake. Was I really listening to God when I married this person?" Thoughts like that come, and when resisted, go. But for two people already aware that society views their marriage as shaky, these thoughts can have added strength. It's surprising how racist such thinking can get: "She's so loud. So's her mother. All black women are loud." Or, "He's so cold and uncaring. Just like Mabel warned me, these white guys have no feelings." This isn't Christian thinking, but Christians sometimes think it.

On the deepest level, marriage is a miracle. As Scripture says, two become one. Without losing their individual identities, a man and a woman enter into a spiritual union which requires great sacrifice on both their parts, but offers untold joy. No wonder God compares marriage to Christ's relationship with the Church: "The two will become one flesh. This is a profound mystery—but I am talking about Christ and the church" (Eph. 5:31,32).

The color of one's mate's skin and the cultural background the couple may or may not share has very little to do with a successful Christian union. Honest communication plus the firm, single-minded resolve to a lifelong commitment is the stuff of a God-centered marriage. All that is necessary—and it is absolutely necessary—is that both husband and wife are willing to obey God and grow in faith together, no matter what comes.

"What God has joined together, let man not separate" (Mark 10:9).

6

@#%!&*#!: Cussing

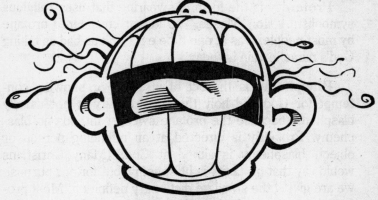

Tom Finley

Why is swearing so popular? Every principal four-letter word, including the "Queen Mother of all swear words" (the *F* word), has been in use since the 1500s or before.[1] Words that in times past were banned from polite conversation are written or spoken in almost every modern book, magazine, movie, and television show. No longer confined to the men's locker room, swear words, profanity, obscenities, and blue language can be heard in the home, on the job, and in the classroom. It is not limited to any group, culture, class, or race. Young and old, rich and poor, educated and illiterate, all share equally in the shadowy side of spoken language.

Why is swearing so popular? Let's find out.

First, Some Definitions

Swearing is the act of using "bad words" (words deemed unacceptable because they have strong emotional connotations). Swearing can be subdivided into several categories:

Profanity is the form of swearing that uses religious symbolism. "Holy Moses," no longer considered profane by most people, was at one time every bit as bad as taking God's name in vain is today.

Blasphemy is the act of insulting or showing contempt for God and holy things. Profanity is not usually blasphemy because the profane swearer intends no blasphemy. Profanity is directed at an offending person or object, blasphemy is aimed at God. (Many Christians would say that profanity is blasphemy, but for our purpose we are giving the standard dictionary definition. Most profane swearers would deny that they intended blaspheming God.)

Obscene language is the form of swearing using indecent words such as the names of certain parts of the body. By conventional definition, the majority of four-letter swear words are obscenities because they make reference to these parts of the body or their functions. Interestingly, most if not all of the principal four-letter words started out as perfectly proper and acceptable English. Only as the years and generations went by did these words slip into disrepute. This brings us to an important consideration:

It's Not the Words, It's the Meanings

Words evolve. Or rather, their meanings evolve. Almost any word you can name has an interesting history of changing definitions and shadings of sense.

Take the word "punk," for example. Originally it was slang for "prostitute."[2] But since then, it has at different times been defined as *nonsense,* an *inexperienced person,* a *burning rope,* a *petty gangster,* a *youth used as a homosexual partner,* and (among many other things) a *fashion style* inspired by punk rock.

When we speak of swearing, then, we speak more of attitudes conveyed than the actual words used. There can be more emotional content, more pure vulgarity, in a young child's simple, "Oh, darn," than the vilest curse spoken casually and habitually by the experienced adult swearer. It's all in the attitude.

Now let's return to our original question.

Why Is Swearing So Popular?

To arrive at an answer, we must first take a look at why people swear.

Frustration is a chief cause of swearing. Frustration can be defined as an awareness that a desired goal has been blocked or defeated. If you've ever had a flat tire or a dead battery when you are in a rush to an important engagement, you know all about blocked goals and frustration.

Frustration leads to aggressive anger. If frustration and anger are caused by our relationship with another person, we need to talk to that person in order to resolve the problem. But when our anger involves an inanimate object such as a car or keys, conversation with the offending object won't help. This kind of anger requires emotional release and the release can come in several forms: acts of violence (kicking in the car door, a decidedly unacceptable response); tears (not acceptable if you are a truck driver); or swearing—the only emotional release that most people find reasonably acceptable. Violence and tears can be embarrassing, and are therefore not usually accepted. (Please note that we are not yet looking at swearing in the sense of right or wrong, we are merely examining it as society today views it.)

Sudden shocks or pain also provoke the swear word. Picture in your mind a pink toe slammed unexpectedly into the unmoving wooden leg of a table or chair, eliciting a violent "@%!&*#@!" from the digit's owner. Again, it is the sudden frustration that causes the response—an anticipated uneventful walk across the room is thwarted, anger rises to the surface, a release is required.

A desire to be one of the gang is also a strong motivator for swearing. If you want to be a part of a group whose members happen to use strong language, chances are you will do so too. This sort of swearing usually has little to do with anger or frustration. It is instead a flag to rally around, a habitual form of speech that serves only to identify "this group" as different from "that group."

An attempt to appear grown up seems to be a strong motivator for swearing in junior and senior high years. Much as smoking or drinking is used by teenagers to appear older and more worldly-wise than they really are. Swearing can be a mask to hide behind, a makeup to wear.

There are other reasons people swear. But the thing

that perhaps makes swearing so popular is its *universality*.
A "good" swear word or phrase can be applied to practically any situation! Want to appear grown up? Throw a
four-letter word into your conversation. You can hype
yourself into believing that your innocent chums, unblem-
ished by obscene thinking, will stand in rapt amazement at
your undeniable sophistication and savoir faire. Angry at
your flat tire? Use that same four-letter word. Stub your
toe? Let off steam with that very same word. The tax man
has just taken all you got? Again, the word. Describes him
to a *T*.

Nothing else is as universal as swearing. Tears might
work when you stub your toe, but weeping definitely
won't make you appear grown up in the eyes of your pals.
Throwing a lug wrench down the street might help you
unwind over a flat tire, but throwing a lug wrench at the
tax man will land you in jail. Only swearing fits every occasion.

Frustrated people need some form of emotional
release. Swearing is a way to release pent-up emotions. It
is the most universally accepted way of releasing emotions. And that is why swearing is so popular.

But Is It Right?

The Bible makes it very clear that swearing is not
right. Ephesians 5:4 says, "And *there must be no* filthiness
and silly talk, or coarse jesting, which are not fitting, but
rather giving of thanks" *(NASB)*. Ephesians 4:29 tells us:
"Do not let any unwholesome talk come out of your
mouths, but only what is helpful for building up others
according to their needs, that it may benefit those who listen."

There are other verses in a similar vein. Most people

recognize the value of these Scriptures, but the teaching is sometimes difficult to follow. The unhappy truth is that swearing is a very tough habit to break. This is what James 3:7-10 says about the problem: "All kinds of animals, birds, reptiles and creatures of the sea are being tamed and have been tamed by man, but no man can tame the tongue. It is a restless evil, full of deadly poison. With the tongue we praise our Lord and Father, and with it we curse men, who have been made in God's likeness. Out of the same mouth come praise and cursing. My brothers, this should not be."

So now we come to the heart of the dilemma. The Bible makes it clear that swearing is wrong. Yet we all— even we Christians—often need a good outlet for pent-up emotions, a need that swearing seems to serve so well. As we think about the solution to swearing, please keep one thing in mind. Swearing provides a *needed* emotional release. The swearing isn't needed, but the release is. It is no good to simply stop swearing. The emotional release must be provided by something. Our answer, then, is not abstinence but *replacement*—something beyond swearing.

Beyond Swearing

You've lost your car keys. One more time late to work and you're canned. But the keys are gone. As the clock on the wall slowly ticks the seconds away, as the minute hand gradually approaches the final moments, you run madly around the house, searching and researching every possible crack, crevice, cushion and corner for those keys. Those stupid keys. Those &%*#!@$%#! keys! That $&*#$%#! job! That @#&*!#%&@+ boss!

Feel better? Perhaps. But maybe there's a better way to relieve the frustration and anger. The best way, of course, is to find the keys. But until you do, the Bible has something else that can take the place of the swear words.

Read again Ephesians 5:4: "And *there must be no* filthiness and silly talk . . . but rather giving of thanks."

The *giving of thanks?* Ridiculous! How can we possibly expect to replace bad language with thanksgiving? How can we vent our frustrations with a thankful attitude rather than anger?

The reason so many Christians have fallen into the habit of swearing when frustrated instead of giving thanks is that they have a very limited understanding of what thanksgiving is all about. In fact, modern Christianity has largely misunderstood the entire concept and reality of *prayer,* of which thanksgiving is just a part.

So many of us define prayer as communication between us and God, as words and thoughts exchanged. Yes, but prayer is so much more than that. Real prayer is a deeply mystical relationship between an individual and the most holy, powerful, and loving Being in and over the universe. The sheer greatness of the forces involved in that relationship is beyond our comprehension. The depth and riches of our communion with Him far exceed any petty problem we face here on earth.

It is hard to understand the nature of such a relationship, more difficult to describe it, because there is *no analogy in this world.* There is nothing to compare it to. Do you have an intense love for another person? That love is nothing compared to the white hot light of God's love, which can be felt in prayer. Are you happy—bubbling over with laughter and joy because of some great good fortune? That's nothing compared to the incredible experience of true communion with the Lord of Everything. Does all this sound a bit absurd? If so, only because it is so out of reach for most Christians. And that is what is wrong with Chris-

tianity today. It is devoid of reality—or nearly so. Famous
Christians build expensive "Prayer Towers" and ornate
monuments to the power of prayer—and then spend all
their time asking for money to pay for these things. What a
waste of prayer!

When Paul wrote the words of Ephesians 5:4, he was
talking about a different kind of thanksgiving. A kind that
comes from a heart transformed by the renewing power of
God. A transformation that comes from a life completely
bound to the Lord and His teachings. This sort of dedica-
tion and devotion is rare. Perhaps that is why swearing is
more common than thanksgiving.

Like swearing, prayer is universal. It can apply to any
situation. Your tire is flat? Thank the Lord that He gave
you a car in the first place and rest in the comfort of His
loving concern. Tax man got you down? Thank God you've
got a job and take comfort in the fact that nobody collects
taxes in heaven.

We become angry and frustrated because we feel inef-
fectual. If those keys cannot be found, there is nothing we
can do about it. We are powerless. We can only hope they
turn up. But prayer changes that. Through prayer (that
established, intense relationship with God) we come in
contact with the Source of all power. God is effectual. Ask
Him to find the keys, remind you where they are, or come
up with an entire new solution. Don't forget, getting into
your car and getting to your job may not be as important in
God's eyes as getting down on your knees.

Again, this kind of prayer is different from the stale,
boring "garden variety" style of prayer many of us have
grown accustomed to. A true moment of touching God is
far more emotionally satisfying than weeping, acts of violence, or swearing.

What about people who swear because they desire to

be one of the gang? As said before this is also a common reason for swearing. It's not a good reason, however. At least not for the Christian who truly wants to be the person God wants him or her to be.

You are known by the type of people you hang out with. While it's fine to have non-Christian friends, your close circle of buddies should be Christians. If you and your Christian friends are in the habit of thinking about and discussing the good things of life, the positive things, you'll find that your old habit of casual swearing (meaning using swear words in the course of casual conversation) will disappear. The good replaces the bad when you fill your heart with the good things God has given us.

This same principle of good replacing bad applies to swear words shouted because of sudden pain. The story is told of Billy Graham, the famous evangelist, who appeared on a well-known television talk show. Talking about foul language, the host of the show said, "Come on, Billy. Admit it. When you hit your thumb with a hammer, what really is the first word that comes out of your mouth?" The host and the audience were pleasantly surprised when Billy said, "Ouch!"

For Those of Us Who Aren't Perfect

It takes time to break a bad habit. And it certainly takes a lot of time and effort to develop the kind of prayer life/close relationship with God that I have spoken of in this chapter. So what happens to us weak souls who still swear when angry, hurt, or frustrated? Is there hope for us?

Absolutely. Swearing is a sin, and a sin can be forgiven. If you blow it, confess your problem to God. True confession and the feeling of forgiveness and cleanliness which should follow can be a tremendous emotional release.

Notes
1. Ashley Montagu, *The Anatomy of Swearing* (New York: The Macmillan Company, 1967), pp. 307,315-318.
2. Webster's New Collegiate Dictionary, 9th ed., s.v. "punk."

But now you must rid yourselves of all such things as these: anger, rage, malice, slander, and filthy language from your lips. Colossians 3:8

Other Bible Passages You May Wish to Study

Blasphemy:
Leviticus 24:10-16

Unclean speech:
Matthew 15:18,19

Controlling speech:
James 1:26; 3:7-12; 1 Peter 3:10

Living to please God:
Philippians 2:14,15; 4:1,7

Anger:
James 1:19-21

How Christians should speak:
Colossians 4:6

Thanksgiving and prayer:
Philippians 4:6,7

7

Divorce:
Is It an Option?

Rick Bundschuh

Before you start to read this chapter, flip a coin. Call heads or tails before it lands. Perhaps you will call the toss correctly, perhaps you won't. But the odds that you will win that game are just about the same as the odds that your eventual marriage will end in divorce: 50/50.

Unfortunately, being a Christian does not seem to improve divorce statistics dramatically.

Something has gone wrong—desperately wrong. And whether we want to face it or not, in our culture, getting married, and staying married to the same partner, is pretty much a matter of chance.

This is not a pessimistic statement designed to douse the hopes and dreams of people who desire to be married. It is a dose of realism so that we can be better prepared to give and keep one of the most sacred promises that a person can make.

Since humans began walking the earth there has been marriage. But what marriage was then or even a hundred years ago is not what marriage is today. The "modern" (and perverted) view of marriage likens it to a contract that can be amended or ended at a later date. To this contract the condition "as long as we both shall love" may be added to replace the old-fashioned phrase "as long as we both shall live." This implies that the couple agrees to share all things mutually until one or the other no longer wants to continue in the relationship. Then, they simply file the proper documents in court and they are let out of the contract, much the same way that a person terminates a lease on a car or breaks with a business partner. They are then free to make another marriage contract with another person. This contract can be made as many times as they deem it necessary for their own personal happiness.

Of course in the so-called modern way of thinking, property, friends, and children are divided up between the two former lovers and everybody lives happily ever after. Right?

Wrong. People, especially children, don't subdivide nicely like pieces of property.

Viewing marriage as a temporary contract has caused countless tales of misery. This attitude grinds up victims in its path. Many of you holding this book are among those whose lives have been disrupted by the chaos of divorce. Most people suffer when divorce touches their lives. The only ones who really gain anything are the lawyers.

Marriage, and the easy demise of it, has become a tangled issue for many Christians. On one hand they have a strong belief that divorce is wrong, but on the other hand their churches are filled with many people who have or will experience it.

The response of the Church to divorce has been wide and varied. In some circles it has been treated like it didn't exist. The pastor and the congregation seem to stick their heads in the sand, ignoring it. The other extreme is to heap blame on the suffering parties, effectively amputating from the Body of believers anyone who has been involved in a divorce. Other Christians have decided to "update" their view of divorce. They have essentially taken the position that the secular world has taken: divorce is unpleasant, but things like that just happen.

Many Christians are still groping to find what they really feel is the right position on the subject of divorce. They are looking for clear guidelines on how they should treat people who are divorced. The following true stories demonstrate how lack of clear direction affects lives.

Sandra was a devout Christian who had struggled for years to keep peace with her husband, a nominal church attender. One day her husband announced that he no longer believed in God. Since he no longer felt any need to obey God, he decided that he was going to move out of the family home. Then, he reasoned, he could really be "free."

Sandra was in shock but tried to keep the doors open for reconciliation. Her estranged husband occasionally came around dropping hints that he was changing his mind about leaving his family. The next moment, however, he would be bragging about the women he had picked up in bars.

After almost a year of her husband's absence and unfaithfulness, Sandra filed for a divorce. The action seemed to relieve her husband of his guilt. He made a point of telling his friends, "She says she's a Christian and that she doesn't believe in divorce. But as you can see, she is divorcing me." He made no attempt at reconciliation during the six months waiting period prior to the divorce being final.

Ron, an active member of his church, was stunned to discover that his wife was having an affair with the husband of another church member. When confronted, Ron's wife packed her bags and moved into an apartment with her boyfriend. She filed for a divorce despite Ron's pleas for reconciliation. Her boyfriend also filed for divorce. Both of the adulterers left young children behind.

Ron now raises his children alone. His ex-wife and her boyfriend eventually split up. Of the four adults involved in this disaster, only Ron is still attending any kind of Christian fellowship.

While these may seem the kind of nightmares that soap operas are made of, they are actual cases from one adult Sunday School class of a medium-sized evangelical church. These divorces plus one other case of a mother deserting her husband and three small children all happened within one year. Astonishingly, the church did not intervene in any of the cases (a few concerned members did, but no official representative from the church). The board members and staff took a passive role, as if waiting to see the outcome.

Even for trained adult men and women, divorce presents awkward situations. If we get involved we are afraid that we may be stepping on toes or invading someone's privacy. But while Christians with good intentions hesitate, members of Christ's Body are twisting and turning through the grueling torture of divorce without much help from their spiritual leaders.

To begin to untangle the knot of divorce we must first consider what marriage is all about and what role God and His Word play in the process.

It has been said that no one gets married for the right reasons. There is a bit of truth in this statement. Some people get married to escape a bad home. Others marry in an attempt to find security. Still others may be forced to marry by an unwanted pregnancy. But most of these people are also getting married because they desire the companionship of the person they are marrying. They do not want to be alone.

Companionship is not a bad reason to marry. In fact it is the reason that God gave for creating a kind of human other than the male variety. "It is not good for the man to be alone," God said (Gen. 2:18). Companionship is the primary reason for two people to get married.

But a marriage is made up of more than two people. It involves another; it involves God.

C.S. Lewis in his book *Mere Christianity* draws a definite distinction between a marriage involving God and one which is simply a civil ceremony. Lewis commented, "There ought to be two distinct kinds of marriage: one governed by the State with rules enforced on all citizens, the other governed by the Church with rules enforced by her on her own members. The distinction ought to be quite sharp, so that a man knows which couples are married in a Christian sense and which are not."[1]

Marriage in the eyes of a Christian involves God because we believe that He designed it as a primary element of all society. We believe that marriage is His idea and therefore subject to His rules and guidelines. Because non-Christians do not acknowledge this basic concept, they cannot be expected to bring their lives into line with it.

This fact is one of the main reasons why the Bible forbids those who believe in Christ to marry those who do not share the same faith (2 Cor. 6:14). A Christian who marries a non-Christian will start his or her married life on a faulty premise. The Christian at least professes to have lines, rules, and margins that have been immovably set by an eternal God. The non-Christian may start with a very similar set of ideas, but because his or her rules are only fixed by what seems to be best at the time, he or she can change the rules to fit wishes or moods without warning or even explanation. It is easy to see how this can affect the long-term quality of any relationship.

Many falsely assume that love will change the unbeliever or weak believer in time. Nothing could be further from the truth. Divorce courts are littered with the remains of marriages that blew apart from major problems that were apparent right from the start of the marriage. The good intentions of one of the parties will not change the other party. It is only by free will and choice that any unbeliever comes to know God and His ways.

When God created marriage He created it to be permanent—lasting for the lives of the two lovers. Jesus declared, "What God has joined together let man not separate" (Matt. 19:6). We have come a long way in perverting God's design with our trendy thinking and disposable relationships. But what steps can we take to avoid divorce?

For one thing, each Christian must not enter into the marriage relationship lightly. Before we make that permanent commitment we should ask ourselves questions such as these:

- Would I stick by my lover if he (or she) had a serious illness that left him (her) confined to a wheelchair or bed for life?

- Would I look elsewhere if that handsome (or pretty) face became deformed through disease or a horrible accident?
- Would I weather mental illness, the death of a child, unemployment, and bill collectors without seeking greener pastures?
- Would I stick with him (her) after time and gravity have taken their toll? Or would I be tempted to trade him (her) in on a newer model?
- Is my desire to marry based on the love, companionship, and respect I feel for my beloved, or on something else?
- Have we discussed the important issues of faith, children, and what we will expect of each other in the marriage?

Real marriage involves real everyday issues. It is not a white horse, prince, and castle. It is lots of fun, but it is also lots of work.

Marriage is a sacred promise made before God. The marriage ceremony is almost always seen as a joyous occasion where the bride and groom want to share their happiness with friends and family. That is why weddings are among the most common celebrations in all cultures.

As Christians, we are asked to obey the laws of the land in which we live. That is why we not only hold a religious ceremony, but also complete the civil obligations of marriage such as taking out a marriage license and having blood tests.

But what happens after the marriage? Once we are married, if things go wrong, does God allow us a way out? Are there any situations where divorce is allowed? Surprisingly the answer is that God permits a way out of marriage under certain circumstances. Not all divorce is sin.

The Bible says that in a very few special situations a person may divorce his or her mate. Jesus gave one example in His teaching on divorce found in Matthew 19:3-11.

Some Pharisees came to Jesus to test Him. They asked. "Is it lawful for a man to divorce his wife for any and every reason?" (v. 3). These men were probably trying to draw Jesus in on one side of an argument that was being waged between opposing groups of Jewish teachers. Some taught divorce was no big deal and allowed it freely. Others held to a much more narrow view.

Jesus sided with the latter. He clarified the situation by saying: "Haven't you read . . . that at the beginning the Creator 'made them male and female,' and said, 'For this reason a man will leave his father and mother and be united to his wife, and the two will become one flesh'? So they are no longer two, but one. Therefore what God has joined together, let man not separate.

"'Why then,' [the Pharisees] asked, 'did Moses command that a man give his wife a certificate of divorce and send her away?'

"Jesus replied, 'Moses permitted you to divorce your wives because your hearts were hard. But it was not this way from the beginning. I tell you that anyone who divorces his wife, except for marital unfaithfulness, and marries another woman commits adultery'" (vv. 4-9).

When the disciples heard Christ's stern requirements they recognized the seriousness of the commitment and questioned aloud the wisdom of marriage: "If this is the situation between a husband and a wife, it is better not to marry" (v. 10).

Jesus pointed out that "Not everyone can accept this teaching, but only those to whom it has been given" (v. 11). In other words, marriage is so serious that we need to approach it with the highest degree of personal integrity.

Clearly Jesus allowed divorce in the case of adultery. The Greek word *porneia,* from which we get the word pornography and which is translated in this passage "marital unfaithfulness," means not just sex with a person other than your mate, but also includes other sexual sins such as homosexuality and incest. Jesus taught that sexual sin was grounds for divorce.

The concept of divorce *is* biblical. As Jay Adams says in his excellent book on the subject, "Let us be clear about the fact that neither is the Bible silent on the subject of divorce, nor does it always, under all circumstances, for everyone, condemn divorce . . . . It is altogether true that God hates divorce. But He neither hates all divorcés in the same way nor hates every aspect of divorce. He hates what occasions *every* divorce."[2]

If divorce is allowed in situations where one partner breaks the vow made to God and his or her spouse by having sexual relations with another, are there any other situations where dissolving the marriage is allowed?

Most Christians agree that the other situation where divorce is permitted is when an unbeliever no longer wants to live with or abandons his or her Christian spouse. This comes from a passage of Scripture written by the apostle Paul in which he apparently tried to clarify what should be done to remedy a tough situation in the early Church. This is what most likely happened: As the early Church grew, many people from households that once were completely pagan became believers. Suddenly one party or the other in a marriage was renouncing the old statutes of an erroneous religion and was embracing a new faith in Jesus. On many occasions this caused great disruptions in relationships. Christian wives or husbands sought relief from their marriages to unsaved spouses. In their old way of life something this drastic would have been handled with a divorce. (Ancient Greek divorce decrees are preserved today and they are remarkably similar to the laws used in most courts today.) But Paul forbade divorce when the unbelieving mate consented to stay with the Christian. In fact, the Christian was told to make the best of the situation, to show love and respect, and to provide a spiritual environment for the children of the marriage. But, Paul said, if the non-Christian wanted out, divorce was a permissible option (see 1 Cor. 7:12-16).

In the same passage Paul recognized the fact that some will not heed Christ's command not to divorce. He gave these people two options: be reconciled to your mates or remain unmarried (see vv. 10,11).

Quite clearly the Bible authorizes divorce but at the same time does so in a very limited context. The real spirit of the Scripture leads believers to strive for reconciliation. The primary call for the Christian in a troubled marriage is to forgive the wrongs of the person he or she married, not to use these wrongs as an excuse to change partners. Even major wrongs such as adultery can be healed with the work of the Holy Spirit and the effort of both parties.

The Bible is silent about many other reasons that people have for divorce. Obviously physical violence or mistreatment are reasons to separate, but again, the objective should be the cure of the problem, not divorce.

Part of the problem with divorce and Christians is that the Church has not been doing a proper job shepherding her people. Because marriage is an act that involves God, it is also one that should come under the supervision of the Church and its leaders. This means that when there are problems in a marriage, the Church leadership should know about it. If one person in the relationship has committed adultery or is considering a divorce, the Church should get involved immediately. Far too often the response of the Church has been to speak in hushed tones about the scandal or to have its leadership sit on their corporate hands as the marriage goes aground.

The scary thing about divorce is that it can happen to anyone who is married. There are no guarantees that the bride or the groom who promised to love you forever will keep that promise. We have all had the experience of being shocked by the divorce of some "perfect couple." This experience brings home the fact that while the short walk to the altar is full of hope and trust, the long walk of life may be filled with bitter disillusionment.

It is impossible to guarantee that your mate will not walk out on you when things get tough. You cannot predict if he or she will drift away from Christianity and begin to think of marriage in the same terms as the secular world. But it is possible, with God's help, for you to guarantee that *you* will not be the one to go back on the commitment you made before God. And in the end it is for our own actions and promises that we will be held accountable.

What can we do to turn the tide of shattered marriages? We can set a goal of keeping our promises to God and to our beloved—regardless of what the future may hold.

Notes
1. C.S. Lewis, *Mere Christianity* (New York: Macmillan Publishing Co., 1952), p. 87.
2. Jay E. Adams, *Marriage, Divorce and Remarriage in the Bible* (Grand Rapids: Zondervan Publishing House, 1980), p. 23.

8

Eating Disorders: Starving for Attention

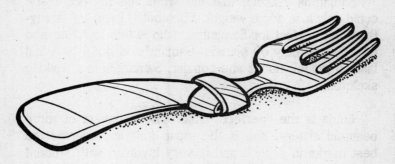

Joey O'Connor

Summer is right around the corner, the latest bathing suits are in the stores, and Jan has just accepted the greatest challenge of her life. The bet she has with her best friend, Sue, is simple: Whoever loses the most weight before school lets out is the winner of a brand new bikini.

Jan doesn't know it now, but this challenge to lose a few extra pounds will cost her much more than the forty dollars for Sue's new bikini. It will cost her her life.

Samantha has always been a little on the chubby side. Surrounded by girls prettier and skinnier than she, Samantha's friends sometimes joke that the only contest Samantha ever won was a pie-eating contest. Samantha smiles and laughs nervously. The playful words of her friends have power—unbelievable power.

Samantha dreams of being a high paid, slender, elegant, international fashion model, just like the ones in *Vogue, Elle,* and *Seventeen.* She wonders, *What would my life be like if I wasn't so fat? I'd be more popular and I wouldn't sit home on the weekends.*

Samantha reasons that life would be perfect if she could only lose some weight. Six months later, life is anything but perfect for Samantha, who is five foot four and now weighs only 69 pounds. Samantha is not a beautiful fashion model, nor is she popular. Samantha is a walking skeleton.

Linda is the "perfect" child. The youngest of three beautiful sisters, she is the most athletic, receives the best marks in school, and is very involved with student leadership at her church. Linda is also a very good cook. Both of her parents work, so instead of her mother doing all the cooking, Linda takes it upon herself to help with meals. She is the "queen of the kitchen." Spending hours after school in the kitchen, Linda prepares wonderful gourmet meals for her family. Delicious casseroles, beautiful salads, and rich desserts fill the dinner table. Dinner is never a disappointment.

Linda loves preparing, serving, and eating the family meals, but gaining a single pound terrifies her. Leaving the dinner dishes for her sisters, Linda asks to be excused from the table and heads for the bathroom. Once inside, she locks the door and turns on the faucet. Pulling her long blonde hair away from her face, Linda sticks her slender finger down her throat and gags as quietly as possible. Up comes another perfect dinner. She repeats this destructive ritual to make sure not a single pea is left in her stomach. Every little bit counts.

Mike was an excellent student. In fact, his grades were so good in high school that he could have started college as a sophomore. But grades aren't everything. Though Mike was shy and scared to leave home, he was eager to fill his next four years of college with new friendships and exciting experiences. The college years are supposed to be the best years of your life. Not for Mike.

Things did not go as planned. Somehow, Mike's innocent dreams turned into a living nightmare. It was our sophomore year of college. Mike and I had been roommates our freshman year and we had developed a close friendship. I'll never forget the cold, windy day in late October when Mike, pale, skeletal, and weak from lack of food, dropped by my room to say good-bye. Against his will, Mike was headed for the hospital. Like Jan, Samantha, and Linda, Mike had developed an eating disorder. He was very sick, his life was out of control, and he desperately needed help.

Do these stories sound familiar? If you suffer from an eating disorder, you know exactly what I'm talking about. Perhaps you'll deny it, but in your heart of hearts you know all about Jan's desire to have her best friend's shapely figure, Samantha's bitterness about being teased, Linda's hunger for acceptance and love, and Mike's struggle with change. If an eating disorder is destroying your life, it is vital for you to know that the pain can be stopped. Whatever your particular situation may be, there is hope, healing, and a positive solution to your problem.

But even if you do not have an eating disorder, it is

very important for you to understand the dangers and why they occur. This knowledge can help you to be a positive influence in the lives of your family and friends, perhaps even helping to prevent one of them from developing a pattern of starving himself.

It is estimated that eating disorders strike more than one in every 200 teenagers.[1] Think about it. Samantha could be sitting right next to you in class. Jan could be one of your sisters. Linda might be a girl in your youth group. Mike may be a close friend who is literally starving himself to death. And you may not even know it. I know I didn't.

Anorexia and Bulimia:
WHEN SLIM IS NEVER SLIM ENOUGH

In this colorful age of high fashion, health food, crash diets, Spandex Running pants and fitness mania, our society has presented the message to the young women that in order to be pretty, well-liked, and successful, it is essential to be thin. (The message for guys may be that they all need to have muscle-rippled bodies like Sylvester Stallone.) In the pursuit of ultimate body tone, we've all heard the health club clichés: "You can never be too rich or too thin"; "You are what you eat," and my personal favorite, "A minute on the lips is an inch on the hips." Let's face it, no one wants to be fat. *Slim is in.*

Unfortunately, thousands of junior high, high school, and college age people have accepted these messages at face value and have developed an irrational fear of becoming fat. Anorexia nervosa and bulimia are two closely related eating disorders associated with this obsessive preoccupation with food and slimness.

According to the National Association of Anorexia Nervosa and Associated Disorders, anorexia is a dramatic weight loss from continuous self-starvation or from severe self-imposed dieting.[2] Through highly disciplined and regimented fasts, anorexics will strive to reach a perfect weight. Despite a severe weight loss, anorexics still think they are too fat. As a result, their goal of reaching a perfect weight is never accomplished. From slenderness to skin and bones, an anorexic's appearance becomes that of a concentration camp prisoner.

The goal of the anorexic is to lose weight. The aim of a bulimic is to maintain an ideal weight. A person suffering from bulimia is caught in a vicious merry-go-round cycle known as binging and purging. In a sick, but realistic sense, bulimics have their cake and eat it too. A bulimic first eats massive amounts of high-caloric food (cookies, ice cream, soft drinks, fast-food, candy), and then through the use of laxatives, diet pills, strenuous exercise, or self-induced vomiting, will seek to eliminate the food from her system. In this way binging and purging satisfies a bulimic's need for both food and the maintaining of an ideal weight. Hilde Bruch, author of *The Golden Cage,* offers a keen insight to this destructive cycle:

> Those who become binge eaters experience it in the beginning as the perfect solution . . . Yet, as time passes, the pride in outwitting nature gives way to the feeling of being helplessly in the grip of a demonic power that controls their life. Gorging on food is no longer a way of satisfying hunger, but a terrifying domination compulsion. Once the binge eating-vomiting cycle is established, it is exceedingly difficult to interrupt.[3]

Anorexia and bulimia are extremely dangerous. Aside

from the complicated psychological damage, both disorders can present serious medical complications. A bulimic may appear to be normal, but bulimia can cause chronic malnutrition, throat and mouth ulcers, kidney and liver damage, rupture of the stomach and throat, electrolyte imbalance, and tooth decay due to stomach acids dissolving the tooth enamel.

Anorexia is characterized by a 25 percent or more body weight loss within a few short months, insomnia, constipation, skin rash, chills, and loss of hair. Both anorexia and bulimia can cause amenorrhea (the absence of menstrual periods), dehydration, and the growth of soft, fine body hair. If left unchecked, anorexia and bulimia can result in death.

Who and Why?

Did you know that a book called *How to Flatten Your Stomach* has been one of the longest-running paperback best-sellers for years? Grab a pile of fashion magazines. Chances are that each magazine will contain articles similar to these: "How to Be Thin Forever!" "Fifty Ways to a Slim and Sexy Body, "How to Lose Weight While Watching TV!" Many women and girls believe these promises, even though we've all been told that there is no magic way to get slim.

In the face of these broken promises, how can we tell who is at the greatest risk of developing an eating disorder? What's the difference between girls who innocently want to diet and those whose lives become controlled by an eating disorder? Knowing some of the signs and causes of eating disorders will enable you to help yourself or a friend in need.

Though the theories and opinions of psychiatrists, psychologists, and scientists differ as to how and why eating disorders develop, seven characteristics and patterns common to anorexia and bulimia victims are:

- *Women*—90 to 95 percent of reported cases are females. Victims may be from any socioeconomic background or race. And, although a person of any age can develop an eating disorder, persons between the ages of 16 and 30 are most often affected.
- *Poor Self-esteem*—Feelings of failure, isolation, loneliness, lack of personal identity, low sense of self-worth and self-control are common.
- *High Achievers*—Anorexics and bulimics tend to be perfectionists, successful in academics, sports, and clubs. The drive to achieve comes not from the satisfaction of accomplishment, but from an over-whelming fear that they may fail or be rejected.[4]
- *Model Children*—Anorexics and bulimics are generally the nicest, most intelligent, obedient, and cooperative children. They strongly try to please and win the acceptance of others.
- *Denial*—Anorexics and bulimics have distorted body images. Bulimics have an inordinate fear of getting fat. Anorexics think they are fat despite their severe underweight. Consequently, they may deny their problem or their skeletal skinniness.[5]
- *Athletic*—Eating disorders may arise out of an athlete's perception that weight loss will improve performance. Athletes or not, people with eating disorders will engage in strenuous exercise to lose weight and burn fat. Anorexics and bulimics spend hours doing aerobics, dancing, long-distance running, biking, and swimming.

- *Major Changes*—The onset of puberty may instill in some people a fear of growing up. This may prompt an eating disorder. Other major changes such as moving away from home, divorce, death of a parent or loved one, or a broken love relationship can unexpectedly trigger an eating disorder.

A No-Win Situation

In doing research for this chapter, I browsed through a few fashion magazines. This confirmed my suspicions about the contradictive messages given by the society in which we live. After finishing reading an article on eating disorders, I noticed that within the span of six pages there were three advertisements promoting Weight Watcher's diet food, a page devoted to Duncan Hines desserts (an ad filled with pictures of luscious cakes, cookies, and puddings), and believe it or not, an advertisement for Dexatrim Diet Pills! Other pages featured perfectly proportioned Athena- and Apollo-like models sprawled across expensive sports cars. These magazines are constantly telling us to eat without gaining weight, to diet without sneaking a few cookies, and to be beautiful even if we weren't born beautiful at all. It's a no-win situation, but something else is definitely wrong: you get the picture that anorexics and bulimics are not the only ones starving for attention in this world.

The media, ad agencies, and corporations try to convince us that drinking a diet chocolate milkshake, buying a new set of clothes, or eating sugar-free candy will make us look like Christie Brinkley or Tom Cruise. Should it surprise us that by giving so much time to our bodies and by paying inordinate amounts of attention to how we look, the clothes we wear, the style of our hair and our performance before others, we may be showing that we are starving for attention also?

Other than condemning gluttony, the Bible does not mention anything about eating disorders. But it does offer great encouragement to those who struggle with poor self-esteem, loneliness, and the frustrating problems of adolescence.

Before looking at three Christian principles that can help both you and your friends realize that *God loves you not for what you are, but for who you are,* let me say this: If you struggle with anorexia or bulimia, please tell someone. A doctor, a friend, a parent, or your youth minister, these and others want to direct you to the road to recovery. Your problem will not simply go away. Eating disorders are serious problems which require professional help. Why let the pain continue?

God's Scale Is Different

In no way can stepping on the bathroom scale measure your unquestioned value as a human being and child of God. Though the world, your family, and friends may judge your worth based on your looks, your grade point average, and how many clothes are in your closet, you'll be glad to know that God uses a different scale. *God values you because He created you!* Imagine that! You are important to God. You have value, significance, and worth because when God created you, He knew exactly what He was doing.

The Bible tells us, "The Lord does not look at the things man looks at. Man looks at the outward appearance, but the Lord looks at the heart" (1 Sam. 16:7). In other words, God is more concerned with what is on the inside than what is on the outside. Now does this mean we should let our bodies turn into obese blobs of wobbly cellulite? Of course not! Our bodies are a gift from God and it is our job to do the maintenance work. God demonstrates His life through the work we do with our hands, the things we say with our mouths, and the feet we use to go where He leads. Paul reminded us that our bodies are precious instruments for God's Kingdom here on earth:

> Do you not know that your body is a temple of the Holy Spirit, who is in you, whom you have received from God? You are not your own; you were bought at a price. Therefore honor God with your body. 1 Corinthians 6:19,20

Good News for People Who Aren't Perfect

Wouldn't life be a lot simpler if we were all perfect? We wouldn't have to worry about zits, bad breath, dandruff, and body odor. We wouldn't have to study for tests because we'd already know everything. In fact, we wouldn't even have to go to school! Though there are people who would like to think they are perfect, most of us struggle with our sins, faults, and inadequacies.

Mark 5:25-34 tells of a woman in Jesus' day who knew she wasn't perfect. She suffered with an illness for 12 long years. She visited doctor after doctor spending lots of money trying to get better, but none of them were able to help her. She was in pain, frustrated, and she may have wondered if her problem would ever go away. Despite all of her desperate attempts to help herself, her problem only got worse. Until she met Jesus. A personal encounter with Jesus changed her life. Read the story. It's fascinating.

The good news for people who aren't perfect is that

God loves and accepts us with all our imperfections, weaknesses, doubts, and problems. John 3:16 is one of the most famous verses in the Bible. In it God promises people who aren't perfect His unconditional love and eternal life in His Son, Jesus:

> For God so loved the world that he gave his one
> and only Son, that whoever believes in him shall
> not perish but have eternal life.

Whatever you struggle with, be it an eating disorder, drugs, alcohol, cheating, or gossiping, know that Jesus came for people just like you and me. Jesus is the good news for people who aren't perfect.

A Masterpiece in the Making

Michelangelo, the famous painter and sculptor, once visited a contractor who sold rough pieces of marble. Walking through the marble quarry, he came upon an ugly, misshapen piece that was obviously worth little or nothing at all. No doubt it had fallen and been broken while being cut. Eager to show Michelangelo his finer, exquisite pieces of marble, the contractor nudged him along. Ignoring the insistence of the contractor, the great sculptor stopped and stood silently before the chipped and worthless hunk of stone. After deep thought, Michelangelo quietly said, "I will take it. There is an angel trapped within this stone and I must release it."

Did you know that you are a masterpiece in the making? If you struggle with an eating disorder, you probably feel scared and trapped inside your body. It's okay not to be perfect. God isn't finished with you yet. A work of art takes time. God is pleased to carve, sculpt, and mold you into His beautiful creation. David, the young boy who killed Goliath and later became king of Israel knew that he was a masterpiece in the making when he wrote in Psalm 139:

> For you created my inmost being;
> you knit me together in my mother's womb.
> I praise you because I am fearfully and wonder-
> fully made;
> Your works are wonderful,
> I know that full well.
> My frame was not hidden from you when I was
> made in the secret place.
> When I was woven together in the depths of the
> earth,
> your eyes saw my unformed body.
> All the days ordained for me were written in
> your book
> before one of them came to be.
> How precious to me are your thoughts, O God!
> How vast is the sum of them!
> Were I to count them, they would outnumber
> the grains of sand.
> When I awake, I am still with you (vv. 13-18).

Instead of listening to what the world has to say about what our bodies should look like, why don't we pay attention to what God has to say? Though you may struggle with an eating disorder or know someone who does, by God's standard, you are a masterpiece in the making. And that's a standard worth paying attention to.

Notes

1. Alan E. Bayer and Daniel H. Baker, *Not Just a Skinny Kid: The Anorexic or Bulimic Teenager* (Boys Town: Boys Town Center, 1986), p. 2 [pamphlet produced by Boys Town Center in cooperation with the National Association of Anorexia and Associated Disorders].
2. Ibid., p. 1.
3. Hilde Bruch, *The Golden Cage: The Enigma of Anorexia Nervosa* (Cambridge: Harvard University Press, 1978), p. 10.
4. Bayer and Baker, *Not Just a Skinny Kid,* p. 3, 6.
5. Ibid., p. 6.

9

Suicide: Help for the Hurting

Rich Van Pelt

Jim, the senior high fellowship president, was a gifted leader. As student council president and as an outstanding athlete, his faith in Jesus had become an integral part of his life on campus as well as in church. Jim and Dave, his youth worker, enjoyed a close and increasingly trusting relationship—or so Dave thought, until one brisk fall afternoon when he stopped by the farm where Jim and his family lived.

A paramedic unit with lights flashing parked outside the barn door caused many thoughts to race through Dave's mind. But none of these thoughts were as terrifying as the reality he encountered when he ran into the barn and confronted Jim's lifeless body—suspended from a crossbeam. He was a victim of an apparent suicide.

Jim was one of those students who had everything going for him, "the last person you'd ever expect to do something like this." But things aren't always as they appear. A lengthy and careful investigation into the circumstances of Jim's life in the months and days prior to his death revealed a cluster of personal struggles that could easily have contributed to his decision to choose dying over living.

Being a teenager has never been easy. Few adults, if given the choice, would ever voluntarily opt for returning to the turbulent days of their junior high and high school years. Most of us are simply happy to have survived that particular time in our lives. The challenges of living with a changing body (which usually doesn't change quite enough—or at least fast enough), adapting to the expectations of parents and peers, coping with the uncertainty of future life goals, and handling the immediate fear that they just may not have a date for the homecoming festivities, all compound to produce a level of stress teenagers are not always sure they can handle.

Most teenagers I meet admit to having considered suicide at one time or another. For the vast majority it's a fleeting thought that is dismissed as quickly as it surfaces. But in recent years, an alarming number of young men and women have chosen suicide as a permanent solution to what often are temporary problems. When emotions overwhelm a person to the extent that it's nearly impossible to see even an inkling of hope in the present situation, suicide parades itself as a way of ending the pain. The events that cause these painful emotions may spring from situations like failing a crucial exam and assuming that it precludes being accepted by the Ivy League school of one's dreams; choosing against abortion when it means losing a relationship with the child's father who wants the baby destroyed; or feeling responsible for the divorce of parents who would seem to have no problems were it not for the teenager.

None of us likes to consider the possibility of losing a friend or loved one to suicide. Yet statistics indicate that few students in America will graduate from high school without having experienced the loss of a close friend or regular acquaintance. As a result, many young people are asking the question, "What can I do to turn this trend around? How do I keep my friends alive?"

Everything we know about adolescent suicide suggests a positive and hopeful answer. Most suicides can be prevented! Studies tell us that 80 percent of those who are successful at ending their lives have first given verbal or behavioral clues that reflect their decision to die. Unfortunately, most of us are too preoccupied with ourselves or unaware of what those clues might be to respond in a manner that could make a difference.

Please don't get me wrong. Some of you reading this have already suffered the agonizing pain of losing someone important to you. The "what ifs" have haunted you day and night: "what if I did this?" or "what if I did that?" The last thing you need is more guilt.

Not one of us is always able to protect those we love from making decisions that will damage their emotional or physical well-being. Responsible parents struggle on a daily basis with the tension between protecting their children too little or too much. There are times when parents err in both directions.

When we feel as if we've "failed" a friend or family member it's important to talk the matter through with someone we trust who can help us gain some perspective.

Once we've admitted that feeling of failure and have received the forgiveness of God, we can begin to forgive ourselves. That's the first step in moving on. There will be opportunities in the future to make a difference because of the way our hearts have been softened and sensitized by this present experience.

Clues in Behavior

If most suicides are preventable because certain clues are almost always given, then we should train ourselves to watch for these signals in family and friends.

Changes in Behavior—including sleeping, eating, and dressing patterns may reflect emotional struggles. It is not unusual for friends to go through changes; it's a normal part of growing up. But there may be occasions when you see a pattern of changes that gives you the impression that something's up. Those intuitive feelings based on observance of behavior can be our first "red flag."

Personality Changes—Friends will often pick up these subtle and sometimes not so subtle personality changes before any adult notices them. Obvious withdrawal from key relationships always signals changes that can be either positive or negative.

Recent suicide of a family member or friend— We learn ways of coping with the bumps, bruises, and major hurts of life by observing those who are important to us. This modeling equips us to cope in the future. Unfortunately, students who have survived the recent suicide of a family member or friend might be more inclined to see suicide as their most attractive coping mechanism.

Changes in school performance—The condition of our inner life often affects our ability to perform academically. Urgent demands of the moment like school

social activities, clubs, athletic involvement, or dating relationships may result in a decline in school performance. A
certain amount of this comes with the turf of adolescence.
However, when friends are struggling with issues that
begin to negatively affect a number of their key involve-
ments, it may be time to become more actively involved
with trying to help them.

Problems at home—When things are not going well
at home, friends are more likely to choose suicide as an
end to their pain. Loss of loved ones through death, separation, the pain of divorce, physical or sexual abuse, or
feelings of being unwanted may contribute to a decision to
die.

Abuse of alcohol and other drugs—The same
pressures that sometimes prompt our friends to abuse
alcohol, prescription drugs, and nonprescription drugs in
an effort to anesthetize their psychic pain are the pressures that ultimately prompt a suicide. The sustained
abuse of chemical substances is symptomatic of other
issues that need attention.

Despair about the future—Young people with
physical disabilities or terminal illness may feel that continuing to live only prolongs the inevitable. When Joni Erick-
son Tada discovered that as a result of a diving accident
she would no longer have use of her arms and legs, she
very seriously entertained the thought of suicide. She
explains the utter frustration of being so physically limited
that she could not even do something to end her life.
Other students struggle on a more heady level with ultimate issues like the one articulated so well in the Mars Hill
film, "The Question": "Is there any reason to choose living over dying?"

Preparing for death—When friends begin to give
away treasured personal possessions, start making "final"

arrangements, and even verbalize their desire to die or decision to do so, their behavior is communicating a serious message. This has been called the "language of behavior."

Steps to Take

Knowing and being able to identify some of the more common danger signs has little value if we fail to take action. Let me suggest a few things that should encourage you to take the risk—the risk of caring!

The first step in helping a suicidal friend is to **recognize that you can help.** You can be a lifesaver! In this age of psychiatric specialization, many young people I know grossly underestimate the extent to which they can be helpful to friends in major life crises. Too many of us tend to think that the only folks qualified as helpers are those with a degree after their name. Studies question such a notion. Friends who have no clinical training can sometimes be of more help in a time of need than those with all the degrees and experience.

Just a few nights ago I was reminded of how true this really is. I had just spoken to a gathering of students and their parents on the subject of teenage suicide. Following my presentation, two young men stayed behind to share some things that were weighing on their hearts. The recent suicide attempt of a classmate had caused feelings of loneliness, alienation, and despair to surface in their lives. I struggled to find appropriate and meaningful words of comfort and hope. Another student who had lingered to visit with me began to share from his own experience. His thoughts were much less ordered, his vocabulary fairly basic. But the genuineness of his concern and willingness to be vulnerable seemed more helpful than my polished adult advice. I was pleased that this young man was available to assist me in helping some of his peers.

There will be times when **helping a friend may mean making decisions that may violate certain values we hold.** One of the characteristics of high school people that I really appreciate is the importance they place on relationships. But a strength can also be a weakness. What one of us hasn't had to respond to the following request at one time or another: "I have something I need to tell you but you've got to promise not to tell a soul! Do you promise?" Friends share confidences. Good friends keep them! Most high school students disdain the person with a reputation for being a big mouth—one who can't keep a secret. The question puts us in a potential bind. We want to be available to our friends and we want them to believe that we can be trusted. But an unqualified commitment to such a request might make us privy to information we should not keep to ourselves. It may require getting to the place where we understand that **our first responsibility is to preserve life, not friendship.**

It's better never to make a promise you may not be able to keep in the first place. When I'm asked to promise to keep information a secret, my typical response is, "I can't make that kind of promise. You may tell me something that I can't keep secret if I'm really going to be your friend. Please trust that whatever you do decide to tell me will be used in your best interest." I'm convinced that in the vast majority of cases friends still tell us what it is they wanted us to know; they simply want an assurance that we do not intend to "tell the world."

When people are either so determined, despairing, or desperate that they actually volunteer the information, "I'm going to kill myself," or suggest that it's a move they've been seriously contemplating, we'd better **take**

action and waste no time in doing so. Unfortunately, most suicidal youths are more guarded in what they share and our clues may only be what we observe in their behavior and/or know from their background.

At times our own emotions are a valid indicator that a friend might be thinking terminally. On several occasions when I've been listening to people tell their stories, I've had the feeling, "Boy, if I was in their shoes I think I might just consider ending it all!" It's a gut reaction that could be off base but is worth checking out. Consider the many times you've regretted not acting on a "hunch" that you had.

You're probably thinking, "Oh great, what do we do, **ask our friends if they've considered suicide** as an option?" Precisely! Most of us fear that we'll give them an idea that they haven't already had. None of us wants that kind of responsibility. Actually, just the opposite is true. We're likely to get one or two basic responses—either, "No—it's not that bad" or "Yeah, I have thought it might be better just to end it all!" Both responses provide an opportunity for involvement.

When a friend suggests that things haven't gotten to the place where suicide has been entertained, don't fail to maximize on the opportunity to **practice what I call "preventative intervention."** If suicide really is a "perverse language" as one writer has put it, then the suicidal person is often trying to make a statement. If the statement cannot be made in more conventional ways, the suicidal person resorts to making the statement in a way that cannot be ignored. It's hard to ignore a dead body. In preventative intervention we want to assure our friends that they never need to go to such a radical extent to be heard. My response would be, "If it ever does get that bad, would you promise that I'll be the first to know? I care about you and would want to be able to share with you." If more people felt connected to others who care in this manner we'd probably see far less suicidal behavior.

We breathe a big sigh of relief when friends assure us that they haven't been pressed to contemplate suicide, but we are terrified when they confess that it's an option they've considered. In fact, many of us avoid asking the question because we're afraid to hear the answer. There may be some occasions when "ignorance is bliss," but this is not one of them! Too often we fail to recognize that simply asking the question, or admitting that if we were in similar straights we might consider a number of alternatives, including suicide, can be part of the helping process.

Suicidal people frequently report feeling so terribly alone because, "No one understands. No one knows how bad it is!" We can never know what someone else is feeling. Each human experience is a personal experience. But **we can sensitively communicate to friends some grasp of what it is they're going through** on the basis of what we've experienced. We hate it when others tell us, "I know exactly how you feel," because we know how clueless they really are. No one knows exactly how another person feels, even if they've been through a very similar set of circumstances. But there is comfort in sensing that a friend has an idea of, or is working hard at understanding, what we are going through.

One of my favorite passages in Scripture is found in 2 Corinthians 1. Paul, in writing to the family of believers in Corinth says, "Praise be to the God and Father of our Lord Jesus Christ, the Father of compassion and the God of all comfort, who comforts us in all our troubles, so that we can comfort those in any trouble with the comfort we ourselves have received from God" (vv. 3,4). For years I missed the full impact of what Paul is suggesting. The

Greek word that we've translated "comfort" means "coming alongside." In other words, Paul is challenging Christians to be those who risk "coming alongside" people in pain in a manner that has been modeled for us by God Himself.

If suicidal people need anything, they need those who are willing to "come alongside" them, be a friend, take the time to listen, and ultimately help them identify and move toward resources that can help in resolving the conflict that has overwhelmed them.

Although we need to believe that God can use us in helping friends and family members through a suicidal crisis, it's also important to define what help we can best provide.

Not long ago I stopped at the scene of an accident where the people involved had gotten pretty seriously banged up. My knowledge of first aid and my willingness to risk involvement were apparently critical in helping one of the people make it through the long first minutes of the emergency. I had no illusions about my limitations. I knew how to stop bleeding and could talk with the man in an effort to keep him from going into shock while we waited for trained medical personnel to arrive. However, once they were on the scene, I quickly stepped aside.

While it's true that helpers who are not clinically trained can often be more effective in helping people through an initial crisis, there usually comes a time when it's important for those with developed skills to move in and take over where the untrained left off! A troubled friend may never intend to tell an adult about the struggles he or she is having. But chances are good that an adult perspective may very well be what is needed. Pastors, youth workers, school counselors, and community-based health/mental health centers can usually refer us to professionals who are trained with specific skills for helping in crises.

A friend may resist the idea of going to someone who will "play with his head." He or she might be more open if you volunteer to go with—for at least the first time. **We must be committed to getting our friends the very best help that is available.** We often function as a bridge between their need and the resources to meet that need. As such we can be lifesavers!

After Suicide

But what about those we fail to help, family members or friends who in spite of our efforts to intervene choose suicide, those who kill themselves when we've had little clue that life for them had gotten that bad? The families and friends of suicide victims often report an almost unbearable level of grief. Loss of loved ones is never easy to live through, yet it's a fact of life. We can anticipate that some friendships will disintegrate, family pets will die, and we will lose loved ones and friends to old age or disease. But suicide represents untimely death that rips at the emotional core of the ones left behind. Death always raises spiritual issues. Death by suicide has caused untold grief to survivors who receive various messages from the Church that are supposed to reflect God's perspective.

One of the better books that's been written in recent days on the subject of suicide is a small volume titled *After Suicide* by John H. Hewett. The author takes great care in surveying the teaching of the Bible and early Christian writers on the subject. I agree with the author's basic premise that it is impossible to find anything in the Bible that presents suicide as a sin that God is either unwilling or unable to forgive. Certain Christian traditions have taken issue with this position through the centuries but their concern has been spurred by early Church leaders as opposed to the teaching of the Bible itself.

The Old Testament writings are replete with reflections of great servants of God who felt overwhelmed by the circumstances of life and wished that they could simply die. Some of those men and women of faith actually took measures to end their lives or have someone do it for them. Saul and Samson are classic examples. Samson pulled a building full of Philistines down upon himself hoping that in the process he'd be crushed to death (see Judg. 16:30). Saul killed himself by falling on his own sword (see 1 Sam. 31:4). Scripture not only fails to condemn the suicide, but in the case of Samson hails him as one of the heroes of the faith (see Heb. 11:32).

The only recorded suicide in the New Testament is that of Judas who hanged himself after betraying Jesus. Judas is condemned as a traitor, but his suicide is only reported. If anything, the act of suicide is viewed as an indication of incredible shame, remorse, or repentance (see Matt. 27:3-5).

In spite of a lack of scriptural teaching on the issue of suicide, the Christian church has historically taken a rather severe position through the ages in regards to the eternal welfare of suicides. The Catholic church has been most known for its belief that suicide is a mortal sin—one that cannot be forgiven. Augustine and Thomas Aquinas were early church fathers who were responsible for setting the pace and shaping the perspective that the Church officially holds to this day. Viewing suicide as a rebellious act that defies the sovereignty of God over our lives, they both taught that it was a sin that did not allow for repentance and that could not be forgiven.

For several centuries the Protestant Church has been

heavily influenced by Catholic teaching on the subject. Yet some influential Protestant leaders have also spoken out on suicide apart from solid biblical authority. Hewett refers to John Wesley as being one of these leaders who encouraged the public hanging of bodies of those who had suicided. Wesley also favored dragging the naked bodies of female victims through city streets.

Fortunately, both the Catholic and Protestant arms of the Church have modified their positions in recent years and have adopted a more pastoral approach to suicide. Although Catholic theology still views suicide as mortal sin, the church now allows suicides burial services. Traditionally the Roman Catholic Church denied this sacrament to victims of suicide. The more openly "gracious" position of the Protestant Church reflects the teachings of the Reformation and an application of the grace of God to the condition of those who die by self-inflicted means. There is little question about the teaching of God's Word on the subject of murder. "You shall not murder" (Exod. 20:13) is one of the Ten Commandments. Taking it upon ourselves to end life, whether our own or another's, is sin! But God's grace covers a multitude of sin, and suicide is one of them.

Even though the suicide rate in the United States has tripled in the past twenty years, our understanding of the issue and our sensitivity to the plight of those who are left behind when a loved one or close friend dies often remain in the Dark Ages. Most of the students I meet know people whose lives have been scarred by a suicide. We must see the opportunity for ministry and influence that is inherent in this tragic epidemic.

Surviving the suicide of a loved one or friend is a decision you and/or your friends must make. It doesn't just come naturally. One writer described it in a way that really helped me. Most of us have heard the phrase, "skeleton in your closet." We understand that this phrase refers to something in our lives that we attempt to hide from others—it may be an incident in the past that causes us great embarrassment or an area of our lives in the present that we choose to keep secretive. The author I referred to suggested that a "suicide is someone who leaves his/her skeleton in someone else's closet!"

As friends of those who have suffered loss by suicide, we can greatly assist in helping "clean the closet." The stigma or negative reputation of having someone in your close circle of relationships suicide forces many folks to keep the tragedy a secret. As a result, the closet door is slammed shut and only opened when we have no other choice. Our sensitivity, compassion, and willingness to talk can assist our friends in confronting the skeleton and getting rid of it.

Don't misunderstand. It's the pain, shame, and suffering we want to be rid of and not the memory of a loved one. The goal of helping survivors is to assist them in moving beyond the tragic circumstances of the death to the place where they are able to move on in life. Because we are sometimes afraid of inflicting more pain, we may avoid talking about the person or about the circumstances of his or her death. As in any other loss experience, people need the opportunity to talk it out, to talk it through. Some young people I know think that this gives them permission to ask about the morbid, sometimes grisly details of the incident. That may be something survivors need to talk through but it's an area in which we must demonstrate great sensitivity. There's a difference between asking, "How did she do it?" and pushing for more explicit details when all we want to do is satisfy our own curiosity.

As we take the time required to listen and respond to survivors, we may discover that we lack the knowledge or skills that would be most helpful to them in working through the guilt, fear, anger, remorse, and other emotions that accompany such a loss. We may really be most helpful to them by serving as a "bridge" to other resources. Our encouragement to get into counseling may be just what they need.

Above all, remember the tremendous resource that prayer can be. In James 5:16 we're instructed, "Therefore confess your sins to each other and pray for each other so that you may be healed." What more can we hope for than the assurance that those who are contemplating suicide or those attempting to survive the suicide of a loved one would be *healed*. I recognize that sometimes we simply invite people to pray with us because it's the "thing to do." I'm not talking about playing some religious game. When we earnestly pray for people, our Heavenly Father promises to hear our prayer and act in a manner that is in their best interest. In a sense I'm describing the ultimate "bridge"—serving as a link between people in need and the very same power that raised Jesus from the dead! As brothers and sisters in Christ we have that privilege.

Recently I had a conversation with a high school friend who's feeling particularly bummed about his life. The more we talked the more I realized that I could best assist this young friend by faithfully praying for him. So I asked if it would be okay if we prayed right then and there. My prayer was simple and I concluded with "Amen." Obviously touched, he thanked me and shared that he couldn't remember the last time someone had prayed for him.

Choose to be a friend to those who need you. God will honor your availability and use you to make a difference in the lives of those around you.

Some good resources for further study:
Bill Blackburn, *What You Should Know About Suicide* (Waco: Word, Inc., 1982).
Mary Griffin, M.D. and Carol Felsenthal, *Cry for Help* (Garden City, New York: Doubleday and Company, Inc., 1983).
John H. Hewett, *After Suicide* (Philadelphia: Westminster Press, 1980).

When Friends Tell You They Want To Commit Suicide

Believe you can help! Most suicidal people don't tell professional counselors about their intentions to kill themselves. They tell their friends or people they trust. If you are ever that privileged friend, you'll learn that it is a scary position. You're scared because you care. You may forget that your friend isn't asking you to play psychologist. He or she wants someone to come alongside and understand. That requires friendship skills and a willingness to risk getting involved, not a degree in counseling. However, your primary responsibility is to preserve life. If someone is at high risk, get help immediately.

There's a way to find out the risk level of someone who comes to you. Many suicide intervention programs across the country use a method of assessing the degree of risk called *SLAP*.

Although *no* cry for help should be ignored, the SLAP series of questions gives us a more informed sense of the level of seriousness. A friend who has had a fleeting thought of suicide presents far less immediate threat to himself than one who has a well-thought-out plan and who is intent on dying.

The high risk person shouldn't be left alone even for a brief period of time while you summon help. Contact a pastor, the police, or a hospital emergency room for help in critical situations.

SLAP

Seriousness of intent—Take every cry for help seriously. It's important to discover as quickly as possible how intent on dying the person is. To help you evaluate, ask these questions:

- Have you ever thought of killing yourself before?
- How often do you think about it?
- Have you ever tried? When? How? (Look for an indication of a history of suicidal behavior.)
- Have you thought of how you might do it this time? (It's fair to assume the more detailed the plan, the higher the risk.)

Lethality of method—The method of choice

gives some indication of the level of desire to die. Obviously a gun can do far more irreversible damage than a bottle of aspirin.

Availability of method—Is the method of choice available? How available is it? In deciding level of risk we must consider both the method of choice and availability.

Proximity to help—The young girl who decides to overdose in an abandoned barn far from home or friends should be considered a higher risk than a guy who is intent on cutting his wrist in the kitchen when Mom and Dad are in an adjoining room.

10

How to Handle Your Parents (Without Starting World War III)

Dave Rice

America, the land of the free and the home of the brave. Where freedom of speech is protected, freedom of the press is cherished, and the right to privacy is guaranteed. Yet there's one thing our wonderful country can't do: choose our parents for us! No matter what science has discovered, you and I still have the parents we have. We couldn't vote on it. The same thing is true for Mom and Dad. Although they probably chose to have kids, they too had to take what they could get.

At first it wasn't too bad; you were a cute little bundle

of joy. But then you turned into a teenager. To your parents it was as if the full moon came out and a curse hit the family. To you it may have seemed as though your parents suddenly turned into Nazis. The atmosphere at home may have become tense. Everybody started fighting with each other.

Many books on parenting teenagers are available to help your folks cope with the situation. But few books exist to help teens know how to handle their parents. Through trial and error, you've probably learned a few tricks about how to work with your mom and dad. These maneuvers may be things like who to talk to when you need money or want to use the car or how to get your parents to let you stay over at a friend's house or go someplace after school instead of coming straight home.

Let's face it though, some of the methods you use probably don't work too well. Techniques such as arguing, yelling, door slamming, the silent treatment, running away, and tears aren't always effective. In this chapter we'll look at several ways for you to get what you want without starting World War III.

What Teens Are Thinking

Jane Norman and Myron Harris interviewed more than 160,000 teenagers from ages 13 to 18. They wanted to know what it's like to be a teenager today. They wanted to know what young people felt about themselves, friends, sex, dating, drugs, and school. Of particular interest was what teenagers thought of their parents. I'll bet you'll find yourself in some of the quotes I've listed below from their book *The Private Life of the American Teenager.*[1]

Ann, 15, says, "My parents can never compromise. They say, 'When you're 18 and out of school, you can do what you want to do. But as long as you are under my roof, you'll do what we want you to do. Period.'"

Another 15-year-old objects that his father can never admit that he's wrong: "It's impossible to argue with him. He always has a better way to do things."

Teenagers also say that parents are often reluctant to acknowledge their good judgment and abilities. Douglas, 16, explains: "Last year when the family went on a ski trip, the skis kept falling off the rack. It was a simple matter of fixing something that I knew how to do very well. But do you think my father would listen to me? He never gives me credit for knowing anything at all."

Parents lecturing and criticizing was a common complaint listed in the survey. Sharon, 17, comments, "I get so hassled when I try to talk to my parents. I handle things better myself." Randy, 13, says, "My father gives me an hour lecture if I bring something up to him, so I don't bother."

Sometimes a spontaneous comment from teenagers leads to the third degree by the parents. They begin to wish they'd never opened their mouths. Willa, 18, explains, "They never stop asking questions if I tell them something. They want to know who, what, where, why— lots more than I have any intention of telling them."

When a young person's honesty triggers a parent's anger, the young person is not likely to be as honest in the future. "One time I went to my mom and asked her what I should do about my busted bike," says Gerry, 14. "Another kid had run into me. All she did was scream, 'Why can't you be more careful? You never take care of your things.' I really needed her help. I felt bad enough about the bike and didn't need her to rub it in."

Some teens complained about being scolded in front of their friends or being treated like babies in public. "My dad's usually pretty good, even better than my mother," says Charlie, 16. "But last week I brought home a friend. Since I wasn't allowed out (I was being punished) my dad kicked my friend out. I was furious. He could have said something to me, and I would have told Dave he had to leave."

Arnold, 16, complains, "My mother will take me by the hand, me at age 16, and show me off to her friends when she has a party. She displays me like a pet dog. I hate that!"

And Dennis, 13, says, "Every time we go somewhere, my mother pushes my hair out of my eyes and straightens my shirt. It's so stupid. And she even kisses me sometimes in front of my friends."

Most young people hate it when parents pry into their lives. Carol, 15, explains: "I nearly died when my mother asked my friend whether her parents were still together or if they had split. It was none of her business."

Jamie, 17, says, "My mother and father keep asking me all about my dates. If I want to tell them, I will. I know they're interested, but I just think it's personal." And Betsy, 16, expresses it even more strongly: "I wanted to kill my mother when she told my aunt I finally got my period. It was none of her (#@*&!) business!"

Other kids complained about parents listening in on phone conversations, walking into their rooms without knocking, reading mail, throwing out things without asking, going through drawers, and reading and straightening things out in their room while looking for forbidden objects.

It's no wonder that a survey taken of 3,600 teenagers in Minnesota revealed that talking to mothers ranked 31st and talking to fathers ranked 48th out of a possible 54 options kids have when they get into trouble. At the top of the list was listening to music, talking with friends, day-dreaming, swearing, and watching television.[2] It seems as if most of you would rather listen to music than talk to your mom or dad!

Why the War?

Psychiatrist Penny Smith has said that she sees a variety of problems in teenagers, but almost all have one thing in common: they are all victims of the "War of Independence"—a war she says that just about everyone who grows up has to fight with his or her parents.[3] The battle zones may be going to church, wearing high-top tennis shoes, getting a "buzz" haircut, listening to certain rock groups, wanting more allowance, being able to choose particular friends, or how late you can stay out on a weekend night.

Why the war? Conflicts often come with times of change. When you were little, you needed your mom and dad much more than you do today. They had to do more for you. But now, you can do more for yourself and need your parents less. You are better able to make decisions for yourself. Your mom and dad have been looking after you for thirteen or more years, which makes it hard for them to let go of those strings overnight. You need as much patience with them as they do with you.

Jesus had a similar problem with His earthly parents, Mary and Joseph. When He was 12 years old, His family went to the Temple which was several days' journey from His home. After spending several days there, His mother and father took off on the trip back home, thinking Jesus was traveling in the large caravan with them. When they discovered that Jesus was missing, they rushed back to the Temple and saw Him sitting there enjoying Himself with the older religious teachers. You can imagine how Mary and Joseph reacted—probably the same way your parents would!

You'll get through this war of independence much more easily if you can understand several things. First, your parents have never been parents of a youngster *just like you*. Sure, you may have an older brother or sister, but they're still on the job training with you because you are one of a kind. Imagine being thrown into an important job with no training, no manuals, no six-month probation period, and no school of parenting to attend. That's what parenting is like. As I said earlier, your parents need your patience as much as you need theirs.

Parents have a greater focus on survival than you do. Dad has to think about house payments, car payments, medical bills, paying for your education. He may worry about his job, his parents, and making his marriage work. Your mom is also concerned with feeding and clothing you, raising your brothers and sisters, doing her best at her job if she works outside the home, taking care of relatives, the household upkeep, and much more.

In addition, your mom and dad are going through the middle years of their lives. Their bodies are not reacting as well as they would like them to. Gray hairs are beginning to appear along with a little or a lot more weight. They worry about getting older and fighting poor health, heart attacks, and cancer. They have questions about God, politics, and each other. These years are as much a time of soul-searching for your parents as they are for you.

Parents are also scared for you. They are swamped by the media with stories of teenage AIDS, V.D., suicide, drugs, alcohol, pregnancy, school drop-outs, sexual molestation, and rape. Fears play crazy games with their minds. These social problems are serious threats, but all that worry wears your parents out. You say it shouldn't, but that won't help them relax at all.

All these things make it hard to get through to your folks sometimes. They become preoccupied and don't seem to hear you. Just because they don't hear, doesn't mean they don't want to. Maybe the timing is wrong. Don't give up on them yet. Again, be patient. They are learning too.

Catch 'Em Being Good

A story is told in first year college psychology courses of an experiment a class tried on their professor. It seems the professor was boring, so the class decided to spice him up a bit. The students divided their class into two sides, right and left. When the teacher, who didn't look at anyone when he talked, faced the right side of the room, all the students on that side would act tremendously interested. They would sit up, take notes, and ask questions. In other words, the teacher would feel their excitement and think he was doing a great job. When the professor faced the left side of the class, the students would yawn, sleep, drop their pencils, and generally look bored. After a time, the students found that the teacher would usually face the right side of the room. The students then reversed the procedure, and the left side acted interested and the right side acted bored. The professor's attention gradually shifted from the right to the left. It seems the students shaped his behavior by reinforcing or rewarding him with something he valued—their interest and attention.

This works not only with professors, but also with parents. There is a saying in psychology that if you want to increase a specific behavior you must reinforce it. That is, when somebody does something you like, reward him.

When training a dog, you use special treats and lots of praise when he does what you want. When you do what your parents want, they may praise you or give you special privileges. If they give you dog treats though, you've got a problem!

We all like to feel important and special. These feelings don't stop when we grow up. Your mom and dad still want to feel that you like what they do for you. They need reinforcements and rewards just like you and I do. If you want to learn how to handle your parents, you must follow some basic psychological principles:

First, **decide what you want them to do.** It may be that you want them to stop yelling at you or to increase your allowance. Perhaps you'd like to stay up later or do more things with your dad. Whatever it is, be sure it is a behavior that you can see, hear, or count. That is, you must be able to know when they are doing what you want. Psychologists call this "pinpointing behaviors." If you want them to be nice to you, that's difficult to nail down. What does "be nice" mean? But if you want them to listen to you when you talk, then you can easily pinpoint their behavior. It's something you can see when they are doing it, you can hear their silence, and you can count the number of times they listen to you with full attention.

The second step is to **help them feel they're getting something.** In all deals or bargains, we like to feel we are getting something without having to give up a whole lot. Swap meets are big in Southern California. People shop there because they believe the deals are better than anywhere else. It's not always true, but people need to believe it is. They need to feel they are getting something and giving up very little. The same holds true with Mom and Dad. If you want to stay out later on Saturday night, what are you going to give them? What would it take to make them feel they are getting something from you? It might be that you would get up on time for church the next day, or give them a quick phone call at a certain time during the evening. Whatever it is, decide what you will give them when you ask for something. You might say something like, "I'd like to stay out an hour later this Saturday night. I realize my curfew is midnight, but this is a special date. I know you are concerned that I get up on time for church. I will be up and ready to go. May I stay out one hour later?"

A third principle in getting what you want is to **answer as many questions as you can** *before* **your parents ask you.** They need to feel you've thought through all the details beforehand. That way they can relax and feel confident you can take care of yourself. For instance, using the above example you could also say, "We are going out to eat at six at _____, and then we'll be going to the show at the mall. The movie is _____ and starts at _____. It's over at _____. Then we want to go over to Jim's house until 12:45. His parents will be home and you can call them if you'd like. And, by the way, I have my own money." Now I know most of you reading this are choking with laughter, but try it several times. You'll be amazed at how your parents react. It may feel like you are telling them too much, but it's more often telling them too little that gets you burned. The real kickback will be that your parents will begin to trust you more and will let you out of your prison a few more times per month. And after a consistent dose of information each time, you'll also find them asking fewer questions and needing to hear fewer details from you. They will have confidence you have thought it all through beforehand.

The fourth step is to **reward or reinforce the behavior you want.** For small children, lots of praise, candy, and TV time are examples of effective reinforcers. While your mom and dad may not respond to you giving them M & M's each time they do what you want, praise, encouragement, and hugs work wonders. Using the example above, if your parents let you stay out that extra hour, tell them thanks before you go out, when you get back, and even in the morning. You might say, "Thanks for that extra hour. It makes me feel good when you trust me." When your mom makes no comment on your room, let her know you appreciate her not saying anything. Or when your dad tells you without yelling to get your bike into the garage, say, "Thanks Dad for not getting on me about this."

Be sure to reward any small steps your mom or dad takes toward the behavior you want them to do. When you train a dog to heel at your side, he doesn't do all the right moves right off the bat. You reward him for each little behavior he does that gets him closer to heeling at your side. A game I've played in my youth group demonstrates this idea of rewarding small steps very clearly: you send someone in your group out of the room. The rest of you pick a behavior you'd like him to do, such as untie his shoe or scratch his head. When he comes back in, you have him stand in front of the group. He is not told a thing but to stand there. Each time he makes a move in the right direction, the group applauds. When he doesn't, the group is silent. He quickly gets the idea that he is supposed to do something and makes more moves according to the applause. In the same way, if you have pinpointed the behavior you want from your mom or dad, each time they take a step in that direction you reinforce the behavior. For instance, if your goal is to get your mom to say positive things about your efforts in school instead of ragging on you all the time, each time she does not comment you could say, "Mom, thanks for not getting on me about my homework. I'm trying harder to keep it up." You could reinforce her behavior when she smiles as she looks in to see if you're doing the work. When she finally does say something that's positive, you've got what you wanted. Any step she takes toward your goal is to be reinforced. Remember, if you like it reward it!

The Plan, The Plan!

Let's put the whole plan of how to handle your parents into a nutshell:

A. Describe the behavior you want from your mom, dad, or both (turning the TV off when you want to talk, increased allowance, talking calmly instead of yelling at you with swear words, not putting you down in front of your friends).

B. Give them something (being at dinner on time, cleaning up the backyard on a regular basis, phoning home from school when you'll be late, bringing home progress reports from school when requested).

C. Answer questions before they are asked (think: what are the things they will want to know about what I want, or what I am going to do—who, what, when, where, why, how, and how much).

D. Reinforce the behavior you want (hugs, kisses, thanks, chores done regularly and without having to be reminded).

Now let's walk through the plan together using a problem one of the kids mentioned earlier: parents entering bedrooms without knocking.

A. Describe the behavior you want: I want my mom and dad to knock on my bedroom door and wait for my answer.

B. Give them something: I will give them my word not to enter their bedroom without their permission.

C. Answer questions before they ask: Your parents might ask, "What are you trying to hide?" or "How will we know if you are cleaning your room or doing your homework if you say we can't enter?" You could say, "There is nothing I'm trying to hide in asking this of you. I just want some privacy just the same as you do. Most of the time I'm sure I'll say, 'Come in' when you knock."

D. Reinforce the behavior you want: Each time your parents knock or barge into the room and then realize they goofed, say, "Thanks for being considerate. That makes me feel like you value what I want."

Parents, like you, need patience and love. Handling your mom and dad using this plan will work if you take your time and are as consistent as you possibly can be. Some parents will respond more quickly than others, but everybody responds to the reinforcements of attention, hugs, smiles, and kind words.

Notes
1. Jane Norman and Myron W. Harris, "The Private Life of the American Teenager," *Families*, November 3, 1982, pp. 42-46.
2. *USA Today*, November 16, 1986.
3. Tim Stafford, ed., *The Trouble with Parents* (Grand Rapids: Zondervan Publishing House, 1978), pp. 17-20.

11

Roles: Manliness and Womanliness

Rick Bundschuh

If you've ever gone fishing you probably have had the experience of getting your line so tangled that it resembles a filament bird's nest. Sometimes the tangle comes from casting your line incorrectly. Sometimes it comes from careless handling. But once fouled, the job of unraveling it is one that takes careful concentration. It may involve a great deal of frustration as well. In fact, a lot of times just when you think you have all the knots out, another one pops up and dares you to be finished with the job. Many people get so annoyed that they simply cut the line rather than hassle with it.

Trying to sort out the roles that men and women should have in today's society, especially any roles that are addressed by Scripture, is much like trying to untangle fishing line. It takes concentration to undo the mix-up, the effort may prove frustrating, and the answers may be elusive.

The very first thing we must understand is that many of the roles that people consider to be traditional are not very old at all. At the same time, some of the distinctly masculine or feminine parts played in society have never changed throughout history and are not likely to change at any time soon.

For example, a role that is unchanging is that of child-bearing. God specifically designed women's bodies for this function. Also women are more involved with early care and feeding of babies. Although men may become more involved with their young children due to their own desire or social urging, women will most likely remain the basic nurturers. Again, God has specially equipped them for this purpose.

Roles that are dictated by the way we were created are called *natural* roles. Most people assume that the way things are "supposed to be" is for men and women to be functioning in their natural roles. This attitude is based on common sense and recognition of the obvious differences between men and women.

There are other roles that we may think of as being natural roles but which really are more modern traditions. Many people feel that men have always gone off to work outside the home for hours while Mom stayed home to wash the clothes, prepare the food, and raise the kids. We have come to think of these functions as being the duties that are natural for men and women. Yet they are really the inventions of a more modern era.

A short review of history may help to unravel some of the knots in the tangle of what we consider to be the roles of men and women.

For thousands of years men and women shared responsibility for the same thing: survival. From early civilization until the industrial revolution most people lived, worked, and died trying to force enough produce out of the ground to feed their families, satisfy their landlords, and make a little money for meager purchases. Mom and Dad both were involved in the care and tending of crops, animals, and land. Not only Mom and Dad, but also every child born into the family had to lend a hand in some very hard work almost as soon as he or she could walk. The whole family pulled together.

Life in the cities of this era was organized similarly. If Dad was a woodcarver, he set up shop in the front of the house and the family lived in the back of the house. Everybody got involved in some aspect of the woodcarving business. All members of the family shared in the everyday household duties. Although Mom probably was more concerned with food preparation and Dad more with cutting wood, chores involving the small garden patch and the making of clothing were probably shared. Children received instructions and care from both parents.

Throughout most of history, farmers' children grew up to be farmers and woodcarvers' children grew up to be woodcarvers. Members of the family were stuck with each other all day long as they labored for their survival.

The kings, queens, and other nobility of the period were the exceptions to this pattern. They were the privileged few who had enough money and power to escape the toil.

Then, after thousands of years of this routine, a dramatic earthquake of change shook up civilization. Although simple machinery had always existed, a period of great emphasis upon mechanic inventions began. Machines became much more common and more complicated. Labor systems changed to facilitate their use. The industrial revolution was ushered in.

Factories popped up everywhere. In increasing numbers men left their home industries and fields and trudged off to work in factories or in the coal mines that supplied the fuel for the factories. Men who had once painstakingly carved furniture by hand began manufacturing it on newfangled machines. Those who had carded wool for the family's clothes while sitting by the fireplace at home began laboring in mills over great spindles of thread.

Since abstinence was the only form of birth control, most families were large. As the fathers left home to work, mothers had little choice but to stay home and raise the kids. (Although in the poorest families, the mothers and children were also forced to work in mines, factories, and mills.)

The world became more efficient, regimented, and streamlined as time went on. Child labor was abolished. Workdays were cut from twelve to sixteen hours a day to eight. Vacations, unknown to previous generations, were invented. More and more of a man's self-esteem became connected with the workplace. More and more of a woman's self-worth came from raising her children well and being a good housekeeper.

The world of Wally, the Beaver, June, and Ward Cleaver evolved. Dad went to the office more often than the factory now, and Mom cared for the house and kids. Her leisure time was spent playing bridge or doing volunteer work. It appeared as though everything was going smoothly until one day the roles for men and women came under the scrutiny of some very dissatisfied women. The

Women's Movement had begun. But this did not happen overnight. Nor did industrial revolution proceed at a steady rate in relation to how it affected the roles of men and women. There were ebbs and flows in the course of history. The various duties of men and women switched hands again and again. Women's rights movements gained or lost ground.

An example of how roles changed can be seen in the history of the twentieth century. During the first and second world wars men left their homes to fight on foreign soil. Their absence in industry, along with the acute need for equipment to fight the wars, put women into the foundries, steel mills, and munitions factories. Women occupied jobs that a few years before they would have thought to be the sole role of men. But when the men returned from war, the women returned to their homes and their previous roles in society.

But in the second half of the twentieth century a couple of new elements were added to the social brew. These factors would forever affect how women viewed themselves and their role in society. One of these elements was the invention of the birth control pill. It was effective, easy to use, and could be controlled by the woman. For the first time in history women could control how many (if any) children they would have and when these children would be born. The size of families shifted from large to small.

For many women it was as if chains around their legs had been snapped and they had sprouted wings. Careers outside the home became more of a reality. Although there had always been women who seriously sought an education in order to pursue a profession, they had been in the minority. Usually it was only upper middle class or middle class women who went on to college. Often they were just biding their time between high school and marriage. Now, however, women flocked to colleges to prepare for careers.

Women also flooded the workplace in jobs that did not require college preparation.

The feminist movement encouraged women to examine their functions in society and to change the roles they had traditionally filled. Women went to court to challenge the right of employers to keep them out of certain positions that were filled by males only.

But women were not the only ones who were affected by these changes. For generations men had seen themselves in the role of provider for the family. They were the hunters, the breadwinners, the guys who literally brought home the bacon. As women pressed for equal pay and even more for equal worth, men began to wonder what their role really was. Men struggled to decide if they should try to be the tough guy loner portrayed by movie heroes, or enroll in home economics classes. They wondered if they should open the car door for their dates or if they would be considered a chauvinist for trying to have good manners. What should they call women who didn't like to be called miss, missus, or girl? The reel that had held the threads of what it meant to be a man or a woman was set spinning. As the threads came off the reel they became more and more mixed up and tangled.

Into this confusion another interesting factor has been added: the computer. Many futurists see a return to home industry being prompted by the computer. In increasing numbers, people will no longer have to go to an office to work. Instead they can work in their homes and can hook up by telephone to the central computer systems of their companies. People will be free to work at various hours of the day and night instead of being constrained by a schedule. This could very well reshuffle the roles of men and women once again. If the man spends all day at home plunking on the keys of a computer, or if he can create his own hours, he will be more free to help raise the children. What other changes may come about we can only guess. But the changes that will come through the computer will probably be more significant than the changes brought about by the industrial revolution.

It is into this confusion about sexual roles that most of us were born or grew up. The chaos of voices, feelings, emotions, expectations, traditions, and ideas has both men and women wandering around in a vast twilight zone, searching for a role in life that will make sense to them. People need to feel that there are some things that don't change. For these things they often look to the Bible.

Some traditionalists like to point out verses of Scripture that show women fulfilling the duties of food preparation, house cleaning, and the rest, implying that these duties are ordained by God. People on the other side of the argument point out that these passages simply reflected the culture that was in existence at the time. They were not necessarily prescriptions for women's roles in all societies that were to follow.

The Bible is clear on the concept of the equality of men and women. This is the first knot in the tangle of defining roles that must be undone. But being equal is not being the same. Men and women think, act, feel, and perform tasks differently. There are very distinct differences in their physical strength: while men have more power, women have greater ability to endure. While these traits are general (you may find some women are stronger than some men, or some men are more sensitive to the emotions of others than some women) they are consistent throughout society.

To suggest that men and women are the same is silly. But they are equal in the sense that while different, they have the same basic worth or value. When we understand this idea, we've untangled one knot.

We all know that there are differences in male and female hormones, but studies indicate that hormones dictate more than who gets breasts and who gets to shave their faces. Two women psychologists found that females who had been exposed to male hormones during a certain time of brain development in the womb wound up with typically masculine personality traits such as aggressiveness and initiative.[1]

But there are a myriad of questions that still need to be sorted out. Should women be allowed to have the same jobs as men? Should women be eligible for the draft? What roles should a man assume? What roles should be left primarily to women?

Few people would argue that there is comfort in men and women having different roles. A clear example of this is in dating customs. Most women still want to have the door opened for them, help with putting on their coats, and for the man to pick up the tab for the evening out. Imagine the surprise on a man's face if his date opened all the doors for him, or her expression if he presented her with the bill for a meal at an expensive restaurant! Dating can be tough enough with some established roles and rules. Most people like having these guidelines.

Dating roles are not the only ones that society dictates. There are other roles that men naturally gravitate towards as an expression of their masculinity. Likewise, women seem to get a feeling of satisfaction from roles that are considered feminine. Interestingly, these positions often have little to do with maleness or femaleness and everything to do with how the culture defines masculinity and femininity. For example, in the Soviet Union most doctors are women, a reversal of the way it is in the United States. So, in that country becoming a doctor is considered something that women are more likely to strive for. Men enter into what would be, for Soviets, more manly fields of work. Now we all know that men and women are equally qualified to be doctors, but in the Soviet Union society has tinted the role of doctor a feminine pink while in the United States it is macho blue.

We can untie another of the snarls in understanding sex roles when we see that oftentimes the way men and women function in society is purely dictated by the culture and not by any real differences in them as persons. Cultures pronounce some roles as masculine and some as feminine. There are always those who cross these culturally-defined lines with no problem, pro football players who enjoy needlepoint or women who enjoy racing cars. But dabbling too much in the opposite sex's role is usually viewed with suspicion.

Sometimes culturally determined roles change. It no longer seems strange to have male telephone operators or women letter carriers. Not too long ago the title telephone operator was solely a woman's title and letter carriers and postal workers were called mailmen or postmen.

Sometimes changes in sexual roles are brought about by circumstances. A single father may find himself fighting his way through the business world with the *Wall Street Journal* in hand during the day while spending time with *Betty Crocker's Cookbook* at night. He may have to develop not only the skills necessary to perform his daytime job, but also expertise with an iron.

One more knot is untangled when we realize that a person does not give up his masculinity or her feminity by crossing the role boundaries here and there.

In some ways, however, society is very resistant to change. Even in homes where equality is emphasized, there has been a marked return to what is considered a more traditional arrangement with men resuming the role of provider and women returning to the role of nurturer. One researcher pointed out that it is usually the woman who initiates the return to the traditional.[2] This seems to be a very recent development of a backlash to the feminist movement. Many women long to return to simpler days.

The Bible gives some help in defining the roles men and women are called to by God. In 1 Timothy 5:8, the apostle Paul gave a stinging rebuke to men who professed to be believers but who neglected to provide for their families: "If anyone does not provide for his relatives, and especially for his immediate family, he has denied the faith and is worse than an unbeliever." In this passage and in numerous examples of men in Scripture, we see that men have the responsibility of being a provider for their loved ones. This clearly fits not only with the historic roles that men have always assumed, but also with the current realities of our society.

The Bible does not suggest that women sit passively at home waiting to cook up the vittles. Scripture suggests that women be productive as well. In the famous passage on the characteristics of a noble or virtuous woman, Proverbs 31, we find a woman engaged in real estate transactions and business endeavors that turn a profit. She demonstrates managerial skills as well as benevolence to the poor, caring for the family, and serving the Lord. It is important to note that her husband is considered blessed or fortunate by his peers because he has such an industrious wife. Obviously neither one of them were threatened by the success of the other. This is as good a model for today as it was for yesterday.

Biblical roles are suggested in marriage as well. But a careful study of these roles and the passages will lead one to conclude that the message is more about "loveship" than it is about "lordship."

With all the pressure for men to be macho men and for women to be superwomen, it is easy to get lost in the tangle of roles. The simplest thing to be in that case is the person you are. If you are a guy who enjoys cooking a meal once in a while, don't hide it. If you are a girl who is fascinated by the workings of mechanical things, go ahead and get your hands greasy. Trying to be something that you are not is a great waste of time and generally a big disappointment as well. Fortunately, for both men and women there are plenty of ways to be comfortable in our manhood or womanhood and still be the kind of persons that God created us to be!

As the line defining masculinity and femininity untangles we will undoubtedly come to the following conclusions:

- Men and women are uniquely different and skilled in various areas. They usually are most comfortable when they are operating within their own unique realms.
- Men and women have the same basic worth as individuals. One is not superior to the other.
- Some roles often shift back and forth between men and women depending on their culture, economics, and other conditions.
- Roles for men and women come from natural, God-given sources as well as from society and upbringing.
- Enjoying some of the activities usually thought of as being the role of the opposite sex is not neces-

sarily a reflection on one's masculinity or femininity.

- Being who you are is the most important role you will have to play.

Notes
1. Peter and Evelyn Blitchington, *Understanding the Male Ego* (Nashville: Thomas Nelson Publishers, 1984), p. 28.
2. Ibid., p. 27.

12

Pagan Influences: Do They Ruin Our Celebrations?

John Hambrick

It's a funny thing about people: we seem to need special occasions to give us a break in the routine and a reason to celebrate. History shows that as long as people have been around, we've had holidays and festivals of some sort.

When you turn from the history of humanity to your own history, chances are that you have a lot of memories centered around holidays. You might remember a Fourth of July when you almost blew your hand off with a firecracker or a Halloween when Mom and Dad, Granddad and Grandma came to school to see you strut, in costume, in the school parade. And what about Valentine's Day? Do you remember being in the fourth grade, pretending not to care if that special someone gave you a valentine? If you were like me, even a string of disappointments couldn't keep you from hoping that this was the year that she (or he) was going to drop one of those cheap cutout valentines into your valentine box.

Of course, the biggest and best holiday memories usually have to do with Christmas. I don't think that it is the presents, decorations, traditions, food, or happy people that makes Christmas so great. I think it is the feeling that this special season connects with something larger than life—something bigger than we can even dream about. All the little details of Christmas seem to run together to remind us of that one fantastic, supernatural, real Christmas of long ago.

The Problem

Some Christians are uncomfortable with the way we celebrate holidays and with the excitement they give us. They want us to take a closer look. After all, excitement isn't always a positive thing. A car accident is exciting. But if you've ever been in one you know that it is the kind of excitement you can do without. These Christians feel the same way about some of our traditional celebrations. Some holidays, they say, give us the kind of excitement we can, and should, do without.

Take Halloween for example. Perhaps you've heard of the Druid priests who lived 2000 years ago in what we now call Great Britain. The Druids are the guys who started Halloween. They believed in several gods. One was named Samhain; they called him "Lord of the Dead." Every October 31, the Druids believed, Samhain called together the souls of everyone who had died during that previous year. (October 31 was called the "Vigil of Samhain.") The Druids believed that Samhain put these souls into the bodies of animals as punishment for their sins. The greater the sin, the lower the animal. Also, lots of goblins and spirits were supposedly loose during this vigil.

It's no surprise that the people were scared stiff. They lit huge bonfires to scare the spirits away. Sometimes, they would disguise themselves as goblins thinking that this would fool the real ones into leaving them alone.

Hundreds of years later, when Christianity reached Britain, the Church started a holiday on November 1 to celebrate the lives of the many saints who didn't already have a day set apart in their honor. This celebration, which is still celebrated in many churches, was called "All Saints Day." In ancient Britain it was called "All Hallows." The night before All Hallows many people would still secretly practice the pagan rituals of their Druid ancestors. They weren't strong enough Christians to give up these practices, and yet they believed enough not to want to tarnish a Christian holiday with non-Christian practices. The night before All Hallows was called All Hallows Eve. This was eventually shortened to Halloween.[1]

Now with a history like that, you can probably understand why many Christians have said that while Halloween is exciting and fun, its roots are pagan (non-Christian) and it is at best misleading and at worst demonic. So, they say, how could any Christian with a clear conscience celebrate something so obviously non-Christian?

Let's explore this line of thought. Should Christians celebrate Halloween? If we follow the line of reason that we should not celebrate it because it has pagan roots, our actions will have greater consequences than just eliminating Halloween from the Christian's holiday calendar. To get rid of all of the symbols associated with our holidays that have pagan roots we'd have to do a major revision of our traditions. Obviously Santa's elves and the Easter Bunny would get the boot. But we might overlook less obvious things that would be thrown out in a clean sweep.

Consider the Christmas tree. The Druids are also associated with this traditional seasonal symbol. On the winter solstice (the first day of winter) the Druids used to meet in the forest to decorate oak trees with gilded apples and candles. The apples were an offering to their god, Odin. The candles honored their sun god, Balder. About the same time, Romans were celebrating the festival of Saturn, called Saturnalia. They also put candles and trinkets on trees. The Romans topped their decorations off by putting an image of their sun god at the top of the tree. [2]

But we're not done yet. What about that bastion of patriotism, the Fourth of July? Has it ever occurred to you that the revolution against England, which people in the United States celebrate, might be taken to be in direct contradiction to Romans 13, where Paul tells Christians to be subject to the governing authorities?

So you see, if consistently applied, the logic that rules out the celebration of Halloween must also rule out practically every other major holiday we celebrate, or the traditions associated with those holidays, including Christian holidays. But it doesn't stop there.

Is Isolation the Answer?

If we can only celebrate holidays or parts of holidays that are exclusively Christian in origin, then it also follows that we must avoid non-Christian influences in other areas. Therefore, according to this school of thought, we should only see Christian movies. We should only read Christian books. We should only go to Christian schools. And we should only have Christian friends. In fact, the end result of such thinking is to remove oneself from all that is not specifically Christian.

There are plenty of examples of Christians who have done just that. Often, such a group will go to an isolated area to live by themselves, cut off from the rest of the world. They see nothing, hear nothing, and speak nothing that doesn't have a purely Christian origin. On the surface this might seem like a pretty good idea if one is really serious about following Christ. But by looking a little deeper, we can see a few flaws in this plan of action.

First, people who separate themselves from everything non-Christian have missed an important command Jesus gave His disciples. Jesus said, "Therefore go and make disciples of all nations, baptizing them in the name of the Father and of the Son and of the Holy Spirit, and teaching them to obey everything I have commanded you" (Matt. 28:19).

The key word in Matthew 28:19 is "go." In other words, we aren't supposed to wait around for people to come to us. We're supposed to go into our cultures to meet them. Jesus illustrated this perfectly. He didn't send for people to come to Him in the hills. He went into the cities and rubbed elbows with the people in the streets— something the Pharisees criticized quite harshly. Following Jesus' example in this is very difficult to do when you live in isolation from the rest of the world. We must live our lives where He lived His, in the midst of those people He came to save.

The second thing Christian isolationists miss is a whole bunch of good gifts from God. James 1:17 says: "Every good and perfect gift is from above, coming down from the

Father of the heavenly lights, who does not change like shifting shadows."

Without question, the best and highest gift God has given to the world came in the life, death, and resurrection of His Son, Jesus Christ. But that is not God's only gift to us, although all the others pale in comparison.

God has given us gifts in the fields of music, art, and science. He has given these gifts through many men and women who, ironically, may have never known from whom they received their gifted abilities. But if the gift is truly good and excellent, then its ultimate source is our heavenly Father, even if the gift didn't come wrapped in a Christian bumper sticker. Christian isolationists miss a lot of these gifts. True, missing the gifts won't ruin the Christian's eternity. But what a loss to leave unopened a gift from One who loves to watch His children enjoying His presents to them.

The third thing Christian isolationists miss is a juicy little fact about human nature. The sin these guys are trying to leave behind is following them. That's because the source of sin isn't in our culture. The source of sin is in our hearts. True, sin is expressed in all sorts of ways. But its home is within us. So when we try to run away from it, we are really just taking it with us. Sin might be expressed differently and more blatantly on Hollywood Boulevard than it is in an isolated Christian community. But sin, unfortunately, is at home in both places. In the age to come, Christians will be made perfect. In fact, God is at work on us already, guiding us to the goal of perfection set by His Son. But all of us have a long way to go.

Wisdom and Balance

So, you may ask, what has all this got to do with holidays? Plenty. The point I am making is that Christians should not try to isolate themselves from everything non-Christian because that isn't what God wants from us. Isolation separates us from the non-Christians God wants us to reach. It keeps us from enjoying some of God's good gifts. And finally, it doesn't even help much, because the evil we're trying to avoid is just as much inside us as it is around us.

Therefore, non-Christian holidays or non-Christian elements in Christian holidays shouldn't be avoided just because they don't have Christian origins. Does that mean everything and anything goes? No. It means that as long as we are smart when we celebrate, we are free to celebrate. We can find some good things in our culture's holidays that we should be able to join in celebrating with a clear conscience. But there will also be some not-so-hot things we will have to avoid.

For example, we may find that our culture has all but forgotten the Druid roots of Halloween. Halloween is usually viewed as a time to get dressed up in a costume and have a good time with some friends. There is nothing wrong with that. But if people focus on the occult overtones and see Halloween as a chance to dabble in some sort of occult or satanic ritual, the results are not only dangerous, but also are evil and should be avoided at all costs.

Wisdom and balance are the keys to being able to celebrate in the context of our culture. We must ask God for the wisdom to see where innocent celebration ends and evil tendencies begin. We must ask God for a keen sense of balance to find that middle position that avoids the error of Christian isolationism on the one hand, and the error of unthinking participation in things that are evil on the other hand.

These principles of wisdom and balance might help us

see that dressing up as a tomato or as Gumby on Halloween is simply innocent enjoyment and that decorating a Christmas tree is an acceptable means of celebrating Christ's birth. These same principles will help us to realize that using a Ouija board at a Halloween party isn't innocent enjoyment; that an overemphasis on Christmas presents is not celebrating in the spirit of the Saviour. Speaking to Christians at the church in Rome about a matter of cultural differences Paul said, "So whatever you believe about these things keep between yourself and God. Blessed is the man who does not condemn himself by what he approves" (Rom. 14:22).

There's one last point to make. Some people are stronger Christians than you are. Some people are weaker Christians. Be glad for the stronger ones and try to help the weaker ones. Don't ever let the way you celebrate a holiday cause a brother or a sister in Christ to stumble. It's true, we are free in Christ. But if we use our freedom to cause a weaker brother or sister to do something which leads them to give in to an old temptation, one you might not have a problem with, it will be no holiday for you when you get to explain to God why you thought your freedom was more important than your brother or sister's well-being. And now, with that in mind, let's get out there and celebrate. We have a great and generous God!

Notes

1. D.J. Herda, *Halloween* (New York: Franklin Watts, Inc., 1983), pp. 1-7 and J.W. McSpadden, *The Book of Holidays* (New York: Thomas Y. Crowell Co., 1948), pp. 149,150.
2. Edna Barth, *Holly, Reindeer, and Colored Lights: The Story of the Christmas Symbols* (New York: Seabury Press, Inc. 1971), pp. 16-18.

Food for Thought

Read the Scriptures. Then think about how you should respond to the statements and questions that follow.

1 Corinthians 8:9: Be careful, however, that the exercise of your freedom does not become a stumbling block to the weak.

1 Corinthians 9:21,22: To those not having the law I became like one not having the law (though I am not free from God's law but am under Christ's law), so as to win those not having the law. To the weak I became weak, to win the weak. I have become all things to all men so that by all possible means I might save some.

1 Corinthians 10:23: "Everything is permissible"—but not everything is beneficial. "Everything is permissible"—but not everything is constructive.

2 Corinthians 3:17: Now the Lord is the Spirit, and where the Spirit of the Lord is, there is freedom.

2 Corinthians 10:5: We demolish arguments and every pretension that sets itself up against the knowledge of God, and we take captive every thought to make it obedient to Christ.

Galatians 5:13: You, my brothers, were called to be free. But do not use your freedom to indulge the sinful nature.

1 Peter 2:11,12: Dear friends, I urge you, as aliens and strangers in the world, to abstain

from sinful desires which war against your
soul. Live such good lives among the pagans
that . . . they may see your good deeds and
glorify God on the day he visits us.

1. Christians should not celebrate any holiday,
   such as Halloween, that has its roots in
   paganism.
   - If you agree with this statement, would
     you be consistent, getting rid of all non-
     Christian celebrations such as the
     Fourth of July and birthdays?
   - If you disagree, are there any
     restrictions on what and how Christians
     should celebrate? What are they (if any)?

2. Obviously, in celebrating, Christians should
   de-emphasize things that are clearly against
   God's teaching. But this might be difficult to
   apply consistently.
   - If you reject black cats, jack o'
     lanterns, and bats as symbols of
     Halloween because they come from the
     occultic practices of the Druids, should
     you also reject Christmas trees, Easter
     bunnies, Christmas elves, and
     Valentine cupids? (The roots of these
     symbols are also pagan, although the
     symbols themselves seem innocent.)
     Why or why not?

3. Mardi Gras originated as a Christian
   holiday. Mardi Gras means "fat Tuesday." It
   falls on the day before Lent begins.

Christians for many centuries fasted during the 40 days of Lent (some still do). In modern times Mardi Gras has become a celebration marked by drunken lewdness. Other holidays that have been perverted by excess are Thanksgiving and New Year's Eve.

- How should Christians respond to these celebrations?

Wisdom and balance: two critical keys to being able to enjoy the good things our culture offers, while also growing in a mature walk with God. The first step in becoming wise is knowing God's Word, because it is God's wisdom that counts, not man's.

Fellowship with God—praying for His wisdom—is step two: "If any of you lacks wisdom he should ask God . . . and it will be given to him" (Jas. 1:5; also see 1 Cor. 2:6-16). Step three is to ask yourself, **"Does my choice lead to balance?** Or am I focusing so much on one issue that I can no longer see any other (such as love)?" Another word for balance is *harmony.* God's Word says, "Live in *harmony* with one another. Do not be proud, but be willing to associate with people of low position" (Rom. 12:16, italics added). But on the other side of the coin, there is no harmony between Christ and Satan, between God and idols (see 2 Cor. 6:15,16). We must beware of placing temporal pleasures above God. We must also search our motives. Ask, Is my motive to *set myself above* "those pagans" or is it to *glorify God* by sanctifying myself? Am I conforming to the world or am I transforming and renewing my mind?" (See Rom. 12:2.) A final step is to examine a choice or action to determine if it was a godly one. Look at Galatians 5:22 and ask yourself, **Did my choice result in the fruits of the Spirit for myself and others?**

The Surgeon General's Report on Acquired Immune Deficiency Syndrome

Foreword

This is a report from the Surgeon General of the U.S. Public Health Service to the public of the United States on AIDS. Acquired Immune Deficiency Syndrome is an epidemic that has already killed thousands of people, mostly young, productive Americans. In addition to illness, disability and death, AIDS has brought fear to the hearts of most Americans—fear of disease and fear of the unknown. Initial reporting of AIDS occurred in the United States, but AIDS and the spread of the AIDS virus is an international problem. This report focuses on prevention that could be applied in all countries.

My report will inform you about AIDS, how it is transmitted, the relative risks of infection and how to prevent it. It will help you understand your fears. Fear can be useful when it helps people avoid behavior that puts them at risk for AIDS. On the other hand, unreasonable fear can be as crippling as the disease itself. If you are participating in activities that could expose you to the AIDS virus, this report could save your life.

In preparing this report, I consulted with the best medical and scientific experts this country can offer. I met with leaders of organizations concerned with health, education and other aspects of our society to gain their views of the problems associated with AIDS. The information in this report is current and timely.

This report was written

personally by me to provide the necessary understanding of AIDS.

The vast majority of Americans are against illicit drugs. As a health officer I am opposed to the use of illicit drugs. As a practicing physician for more than 40 years, I have seen the devastation that follows the use of illicit drugs—addiction, poor health, family disruption, emotional disturbances and death. I applaud the President's initiative to rid this nation of the curse of illicit drug use and addiction. The success of his initiative is critical to the health of the American people and will also help reduce the number of persons exposed to the AIDS virus.

Some Americans have difficulties in dealing with the subjects of sex, sexual practices and alternate lifestyles. Many Americans are opposed to homosexuality, promiscuity of any kind and prostitution. This report must deal with all of these issues, but does so with the intent that information and education can change individual behavior, since this is the primary way to stop the epidemic of AIDS. This report deals with the positive and negative consequences of activities and behaviors from a health and medical point of view.

Adolescents and pre-adolescents are those whose behavior we wish to especially influence because of their vulnerability when they are exploring their own sexuality (heterosexual and homosexual) and perhaps experimenting with drugs. Teenagers often consider themselves immoral, and these young people may be putting themselves at great risk.

Education about AIDS should start in early elementary school and at home so that children can grow up knowing the behavior to avoid to protect themselves from exposure to the AIDS virus. The threat of AIDS can provide an opportunity for parents to instill in their children their own moral and ethical standards.

Those of us who are

parents, educators and community leaders, indeed all adults, cannot disregard this responsibility to educate our young. The need is critical and the price of neglect is high. The lives of our young people depend on our fulfilling our responsibility.

AIDS is an infectious disease. It is contagious, but it cannot be spread in the same manner as a common cold or measles or chicken pox. It is contagious in the same way that sexually transmitted diseases, such as syphilis and gonorrhea, are contagious. AIDS can also be spread through the sharing of intravenous drug needles and syringes used for injecting illicit drugs.

AIDS is *not* spread by common everyday contact but by sexual contact (penis-vagina, penis-rectum, mouth-rectum, mouth-vagina, mouth-penis). Yet there is great misunderstanding resulting in unfounded fear that AIDS can be spread by casual, non-sexual contact. The first cases of AIDS were reported in this country in 1981. We would know by now if AIDS were passed by casual, non-sexual contact.

Today those practicing high risk behavior who become infected with the AIDS virus are found mainly among homosexual and bisexual men and male and female intravenous drug users. Heterosexual transmission is expected to account for an increasing proportion of those who become infected with the AIDS virus in the future.

At the beginning of the AIDS epidemic many Americans had little sympathy for people with AIDS. The feeling was that somehow people from certain groups "deserved" their illness. Let us put those feelings behind us. We are fighting a disease, not people. Those who are already afflicted are sick people and need our care as do all sick patients. The country must face this epidemic as a unified society. We must prevent the spread of AIDS while at the same time preserving our humanity and intimacy.

AIDS is a life-threatening disease and a major public

health issue. Its impact on our society is and will continue to be devastating. By the end of 1991, an estimated 270,000 cases of AIDS will have occurred with 179,000 deaths within the decade since the disease was first recognized. In the year 1991, an estimated 145,000 patients with AIDS will need health and supportive services at a total cost of between $8 and $16 billion. However, AIDS is preventable. It can be controlled by changes in personal behavior. It is the responsibility of every citizen to be informed about AIDS and to exercise the appropriate preventive measures. This report will tell you how.

The spread of AIDS can and must be stopped.

C. EVERETT KOOP, M.D., Sc.D.
Surgeon General

AIDS

AIDS Caused by Virus

The letters A-I-D-S stand for Acquired Immune Deficiency Syndrome. When a person is sick with AIDS, he/she is in the final stages of a series of health problems caused by a virus (germ) that can be passed from one person to another chiefly during sexual contact or through the sharing of intravenous drug needles and syringes used for "shooting" drugs. Scientists have named the AIDS virus "HIV or HTLV-III or LAV"*. These abbreviations stand for information denoting a virus that attacks white blood cells

---

* These are different names given to AIDS virus by the scientific community:

HIV—Human Immunodeficiency Virus.
HTLV-III—Human T-Lymphotropic Virus Type III
LAV—Lymphadenopathy Associated Virus

(T-Lymphocytes) in the human blood. Throughout this publication, we will call the virus the "AIDS virus." The AIDS virus attacks a person's immune system and damages his/her ability to fight other diseases. Without a functioning immune system to ward off other germs, he/she now becomes vulnerable to becoming infected by bacteria, protozoa, fungi and other viruses and malignancies, which may cause life-threatening illness, such as pneumonia, meningitis and cancer.

No Known Cure

There is presently no cure for AIDS. There is presently no vaccine to prevent AIDS.

Virus Invades Blood Stream

When the AIDS virus enters the blood stream, it begins to attack certain white blood cells (T-Lymphocytes). Substances called antibodies are produced by the body.

These antibodies can be detected in the blood by a simple test, usually two weeks to three months after infection. Even before the antibody test is positive, the victim can pass the virus to others by methods that will be explained.

Once an individual is infected, there are several possibilities. Some people may remain well but even so they are able to infect others. Others may develop a disease that is less serious than AIDS referred to as AIDS Related Complex (ARC). In some people the protective immune system may be destroyed by the virus and then other germs (bacteria, protozoa, fungi and other viruses) and cancers that ordinarily would never get a foothold cause "opportunistic diseases"— using the *opportunity* of lowered resistance to infect and destroy. Some of the most common are *Pneumocystis carinii* pneumonia and tuberculosis. Individuals infected with the AIDS virus may also develop certain types of cancers such as Kaposi's sarcoma. These infected people have classic AIDS. Evidence shows that the AIDS virus may also attack the nervous system, causing damage to the brain.

Signs and Symptoms

No Signs

Some people remain apparently well after infection with the AIDS virus. They may have no physically apparent symptoms of illness. However, if proper precautions are not used with sexual contacts and/or intravenous drug use, these infected individuals can spread the virus to others. Anyone who thinks he or she is infected or involved in high risk behaviors should not donate his/her blood, organs, tissues, or sperm because they may now contain the AIDS virus.

ARC

AIDS-Related Complex (ARC) is a condition caused by the AIDS virus in which the patient tests positive for AIDS infection and has a specific set of clinical symptoms. However, ARC patients' symptoms are often less severe than those with the disease we call classic AIDS. Signs and symptoms of ARC may include loss of appetite, weight loss, fever, night sweats, skin rashes, diarrhea, tiredness, lack of resistance to infection, or swollen lymph nodes. These are also signs and symptoms of many other diseases and a physician should be consulted.

AIDS

Only a qualified health professional can diagnose AIDS, which is the result of a natural progress of infection by the AIDS virus. AIDS destroys the body's immune (defense) system and allows otherwise controllable infections to invade the body and cause additional diseases.

These opportunistic diseases would not otherwise gain a foothold in the body. These opportunistic diseases may eventually cause death.

Some symptoms and signs of AIDS and the "opportunistic infections" may include a persistent cough and fever associated with shortness of breath or difficult breathing and may be the symptoms of *Pneumocystis carinii* pneumonia. Multiple purplish blotches and bumps on the skin may be a sign of Kaposi's sarcoma. The AIDS virus in all infected people is essentially the same; the reactions of individuals may differ.

Long Term

The AIDS virus may also attack the nervous system and cause delayed damage to the brain. This damage may take years to develop and the symptoms may show up as memory loss, indifference, loss of coordination, partial paralysis or mental disorder. These symptoms may occur alone, or with other symptoms mentioned earlier.

The Present Situation

The number of people estimated to be infected with the AIDS virus in the United States is about 1.5 million. All of these individuals are assumed to be capable of spreading the virus sexually (heterosexually or homosexually) or by sharing needles and syringes or other implements for intravenous drug use. Of these, an estimated 100,000 to 200,000 will come down with AIDS Related Complex (ARC). It is difficult to predict the number who will develop ARC or AIDS because symptoms sometimes take as long as nine years to show up. With our present knowledge, scientists predict that 20 to 30% of those infected with the AIDS virus will develop an illness that fits an accepted definition of AIDS within five years. The number of persons known to have AIDS in the United States to date is over 25,000; of these, about half have died of the disease. Since there is no cure, the others are expected to also eventually die from their disease.

The majority of infected antibody positive individuals who carry the AIDS virus show no disease symptoms and may not come down with the disease for many years, if ever.

No Risk from Casual Contact

There is no known risk of non-sexual infection in most of the situations we encounter in our daily lives. We know that family members living with individuals who have the AIDS virus do not become infected except through sexual contact. There is no evidence of transmission (spread) of AIDS virus by everyday contact even though these family members shared food, towels, cups, razors, even toothbrushes, and kissed each other.

Health Workers

We know even more about health care workers exposed to AIDS patients. About 2,500 health workers who were caring for AIDS patients when they were sickest have been carefully studied and tested for infection with the AIDS virus. These doctors, nurses and other health care givers have been exposed to the AIDS patients' blood, stool and other body fluids. Approximately 750 of these health workers reported possible additional exposure by direct contact with a patient's body fluid through spills or being accidentally stuck with a needle. Upon testing these 750, only 3 who had accidentally stuck themselves with a needle had a positive antibody test for exposure to the AIDS virus. Because health workers had much more contact with patients and their body fluids than would be expected from common everyday contact, it is clear that the AIDS virus is not transmitted by casual contact.

Control of Certain Behaviors Can Stop Further Spread of AIDS

Knowing the facts about AIDS can prevent the spread of the disease. Education of those who risk infecting themselves or infecting other people is the only way we can stop the spread of AIDS. People must be responsible about their sexual behavior and must avoid the use of illicit intravenous drugs and needle sharing. We will describe the types of behavior that lead to infection by the AIDS virus and the personal measures that must be taken for effective protection. If we are to stop the AIDS epidemic, we all must understand the disease—its cause, its nature, and its prevention. *Precautions must be taken.* The AIDS virus infects persons who expose themselves to known risk behavior, such as certain types of homosexual and heterosexual activities or sharing intravenous drug equipment.

Risks

Although the initial discovery was in the homosexual community, AIDS is not a disease only of homosexuals. AIDS is found in heterosexual people as well. AIDS is not a black or white disease. AIDS is not just a male disease. AIDS is found in women; it is found in children. In the future AIDS will probably increase and spread among people who are not homosexual or intravenous drug abusers in the same manner as other sexually transmitted diseases like syphilis and gonorrhea.

Sex Between Men

Men who have sexual relations with other men are especially at risk. About 70% of AIDS victims throughout the country are male homosexuals and bisexuals. This percentage probably will decline as heterosexual transmission increases. *Infection results from a sexual relationship with an infected person.*

Multiple Partners

The risk of infection increases according to the number of sexual partners one has, *male or female*. The more partners you have, the greater the risk of becoming infected with the AIDS virus.

How Exposed

Although the AIDS virus is found in several body fluids, a person acquires the virus during sexual contact with an infected person's blood or semen and possibly vaginal secretions. The virus then enters a person's blood stream through their rectum, vagina or penis.

Small (unseen by the naked eye) tears in the surface lining of the vagina or rectum may occur during insertion of the penis, fingers or other objects, thus opening an avenue for entrance of the virus directly into the blood stream; therefore, the AIDS virus can be passed from penis to rectum and vagina and vice versa without a visible tear in the tissue or the presence of blood.

Prevention of Sexual Transmission—Know Your Partner

Couples who maintain mutually faithful monogamous relationships (only one continuing sexual partner) are protected from AIDS through sexual transmission. If you have been faithful for at least five years and your partner has been faithful too, neither of you is at risk. If you have not been faithful, then you and your partner are at risk. If your partner has not been faithful, then your partner is at risk which also puts you at risk. This is true for both heterosexual and homosexual couples. Unless it is possible to know with *absolute certainty* that neither you nor your sexual partner is carrying the virus of AIDS, you must use protective behavior. *Absolute certainty* means not only that you and your partner have maintained a mutually faithful monogamous sexual relationship, but it means that neither you nor your partner has used illegal intravenous drugs.

You Can Protect Yourself from Infection

Some personal measures are adequate to safely protect yourself and others from infection by the AIDS virus and its complications. Among these are:

• If you have been involved in any of the high risk sexual activities described above or have injected illicit intravenous drugs into your body, you should have a blood test to see if you have been infected with the AIDS virus.

• If your test is positive or if you engage in high risk activities and choose not to have a test, you should tell your sexual partner. If you jointly decide to have sex, you must protect your partner by always using a rubber (condom) during (start to finish) sexual intercourse (vagina or rectum).

• If your partner has a positive blood test showing that he/she has been infected with the AIDS virus or you suspect that he/she has been exposed by previous heterosexual or homosexual behavior or use of intravenous drugs with shared needles and syringes, a rubber (condom) should always be used during (start to finish) sexual intercourse (vagina or rectum).

• If you or your partner is at high risk, avoid mouth contact with the penis, vagina or rectum.

• Avoid all sexual activities which could cause cuts or tears in the linings of the rectum, vagina or penis.

• Single teen-age girls have been warned that pregnancy and contracting sexually transmitted diseases can be the result of only one act of sexual intercourse. They have been taught to say *NO* to sex! They have been taught to say *NO* to drugs! By saying *NO* to sex and drugs, they can avoid AIDS which can *kill* them! The same is true for teen-age boys, who should also not have rectal intercourse with other males. It may result in AIDS.

• Do not have sex with prostitutes. Infected male and female prostitutes are frequently also intravenous drug abusers; therefore, they may infect clients by sexual intercourse and other intravenous drug abusers by sharing their intravenous drug equipment. Female prostitutes also can infect their unborn babies.

Intravenous Drug Users

Drug abusers who inject drugs into their veins are another population group at high risk and with high rates of infection by the AIDS virus. Users of intravenous drugs make up 25% of the cases of AIDS throughout the country. The AIDS virus is carried in contaminated blood left in the needle, syringe or other drug related implements and the virus is injected into the new victim by reusing dirty syringes and needles. Even the smallest amount of infected blood left in a used needle or syringe can contain live AIDS virus to be passed on to the next user of those dirty implements.

No one should shoot up drugs, because addiction, poor health, family disruption, emotional disturbances and death could follow. However, many drug users are addicted to drugs and for one reason or another have not changed their behavior. For these people, the only way not to get AIDS is *to use a clean, previously unused* needle, syringe or any other implement necessary for the injection of the drug solution.

Hemophilia

Some persons with

hemophilia (a blood clotting disorder that makes them subject to bleeding) have been infected with the AIDS virus either through blood transfusion or the use of blood products that help their blood clot. Now that we know how to prepare safe blood products to aid clotting, this is unlikely to happen. This group represents a very small percentage of the cases of AIDS throughout the country.

Blood Transfusion

Currently all blood donors are initially screened and blood is *not* accepted from high risk individuals. Blood that has been collected for use is tested for the presence of antibody to the AIDS virus. However, some people may have had a blood transfusion prior to March, 1985, before we knew how to screen blood for safe transfusion and may have become infected with the AIDS virus. Fortunately there are not now a large number of these cases. With routine testing of blood products, the blood supply for transfusion is now safer than it has ever been with regard to AIDS.

Persons who have engaged in homosexual activities or have "shot" street drugs within the last 10 years should *never* donate blood.

Mother Can Infect Newborn

If a woman is infected with the AIDS virus and becomes pregnant, she is more likely to develop ARC or classic AIDS, and she can pass the AIDS virus to her unborn child. Approximately one-third of the babies born to AIDS-infected mothers will also be infected with the AIDS virus. Most of the infected babies will eventually develop the disease and die. Several of these babies have been born to wives of hemophiliac men infected with the AIDS virus by way of *contaminated* blood products. Some babies have also been born to women who became infected with the AIDS virus by bisexual partners who had the virus. Almost all babies with AIDS have been born to women who were intravenous drug users or the sexual partners of intravenous drug users who were infected with the AIDS virus. More such babies can be expected.

Think carefully if you plan on becoming pregnant. If there is any chance that you may be in any high risk group or that you have had sex with someone in a high risk group, such as homosexual and bisexual males, drug abusers and their sexual partners, see your doctor.

Summary

AIDS affects certain groups of the population. Homosexual and bisexual males who have had sexual contact with other homosexual or bisexual males as well as those who "shoot" street drugs are at greatest risk of exposure, infection and eventual death. Sexual partners of these high risk individuals are at risk, as well as any children born to women who carry the virus. Heterosexual persons are increasingly at risk.

What Is Safe

Most Behavior Is Safe

Everyday living does not present any risk of infection. You *cannot* get AIDS from casual social contact. Casual social contact should not be confused with casual *sexual* contact, which is a major cause of the spread of the AIDS virus. Casual *social* contact such as shaking hands, hugging, social kissing, crying, coughing or sneezing, will not transmit the AIDS virus. Nor has AIDS been contracted from swimming in pools or bathing in hot tubs or from eating in restaurants (even if a restaurant worker has AIDS or carries the AIDS virus). AIDS is not contracted from sharing bed linens, towels, cups, straws, dishes or any other eating utensils. You cannot get AIDS from toilets, doorknobs, telephones, office machinery or household furniture. You cannot get AIDS from body massages, masturbation or any non-sexual contact.

Donating Blood

Donating blood is *not* risky at all. *You cannot get AIDS by donating blood.*

Receiving Blood

In the U.S. every blood donor is screened to exclude high risk persons and every blood donation is now tested for the presence of antibodies to the AIDS virus. Blood that shows exposure to the AIDS virus by the presence of antibodies is not used either for transfusion or for the manufacture of blood products. Blood banks are as safe as current technology can make them. Because antibodies do not form immediately after exposure to the virus, a newly infected person may unknowingly donate blood after becoming infected but before his/her antibody test becomes positive. It is estimated that this might occur less than once in 100,000 donations.

There is no danger of AIDS virus infection from visiting a doctor, dentist,
hospital, hairdresser or beautician. AIDS cannot be transmitted non-sexually from an infected person through a health or service provider to another person. Ordinary methods of disinfection for urine, stool and vomitus which are used for non-infected people are adequate for people who have AIDS or are carrying the AIDS virus. You may have wondered why your dentist wears gloves and perhaps a mask when treating you. This does not mean that he has AIDS or that he thinks you do. He is protecting you and himself from hepatitis, common colds or flu.

There is no danger in visiting a patient with AIDS or caring for him or her. Normal hygienic practices, like wiping of body fluid spills with a solution of water and household bleach (1 part household bleach to 10 parts water), will provide full protection.

Children in School

None of the identified cases of AIDS in the United

States are known or are suspected to have been transmitted from one child to another in school, day care or foster care settings. Transmission would necessitate exposure of open cuts to the blood or other body fluids of the infected child, a highly unlikely occurrence. Even then routine safety procedures for handling blood or other body fluids (which should be standard for all children in the school or day care setting) would be effective in preventing transmission from children with AIDS to other children in school.

Children with AIDS are highly susceptible to infections, such as chicken pox, from other children. Each child with AIDS should be examined by a doctor before attending school or before returning to school, day care or foster care settings after an illness. No blanket rules can be made for all school boards to cover all possible cases of children with AIDS and each case should be considered separately and individualized to the child and the setting, as would be done with any child with a special problem, such as cerebral palsy or asthma. A good team to make such decisions with the school board would be the child's parents, physician and a public health official.

Casual social contact between children and persons infected with the AIDS virus is not dangerous.

Insects

There are no known cases of AIDS transmission by insects, such as mosquitoes.

Pets

Dogs, cats and domestic animals are not a source of infection from AIDS virus.

Tears and Saliva

Although the AIDS virus has been found in tears and saliva, no instance of transmission from these body fluids has been reported.

AIDS comes from sexual contacts with infected persons

and from the sharing of syringes and needles. There is no danger of infection with AIDS virus by casual social contact.

Testing of Military Personnel

You may wonder why the Department of Defense is currently testing its uniformed services personnel for presence of the AIDS virus antibody. The military feel this procedure is necessary because the uniformed services act as their own blood bank in a time of national emergency. They also need to protect new recruits (who unknowingly may be AIDS virus carriers) from receiving live virus vaccines. These vaccines could activate disease and be potentially life-threatening to the recruits.

What Is Currently Understood

Although AIDS is still a mysterious disease in many ways, our scientists have learned a great deal about it. In five years we know more about AIDS than many diseases that we have studied for even longer periods. While there is no vaccine or cure, the results from the health and behavioral research community can only add to our knowledge and increase our understanding of the disease and ways to prevent and treat it.

In spite of all that is known about transmission of the AIDS virus, scientists will learn more. One possibility is the potential discovery of factors that may better explain the mechanism of AIDS infection.

Why are the antibodies produced by the body to fight the AIDS virus not able to destroy that virus?

The antibodies detected in the blood of carriers of the AIDS virus are ineffective, at least when classic AIDS is actually triggered. They cannot check the damage caused by the virus, which is by then present in large numbers in the body. Researchers cannot explain this important observation. We still do not know why the AIDS virus is not destroyed by man's immune system.

Summary

AIDS no longer is the concern of any one segment of society; it is the concern of us all. No American's life is in danger if he/she or their sexual partners do not engage in high risk sexual behavior or use shared needles or syringes to inject illicit drugs into the body.

People who engage in high risk sexual behavior or who shoot drugs are risking infection with the AIDS virus and are risking their lives and the lives of others, including their unborn children.

We cannot yet know the full impact of AIDS on our society. From a clinical point of view, there may be new manifestations of AIDS—for example, mental disturbances due to the infection of the brain by the AIDS virus in carriers of the virus. From a social point of view, it may bring to an end the free-wheeling sexual life-style which has been called the sexual revolution. Economically, the care of AIDS patients will put a tremendous strain on our already overburdened and costly healthy care delivery system.

The most certain way to avoid getting the AIDS virus and to control the AIDS epidemic in the United States is for individuals to avoid promiscuous sexual practices, to maintain mutually faithful monogamous sexual relationships and to avoid injecting illicit drugs.

Look to the Future

The Challenge of the Future

An enormous challenge to public health lies ahead of us and we would do well to take a look at the future. We must be prepared to manage those things we can predict, as well as those we cannot. At the present time there is no vaccine to prevent AIDS. There is no cure. AIDS, which can be transmitted sexually and by sharing needles and syringes among illicit intravenous drug users, is bound to produce profound changes in our society, changes that will affect us all.

Information and Education Only Weapons Against AIDS

It is estimated that in 1991 54,000 people will die from AIDS. At this moment, many of them are not infected with the AIDS virus. With proper information and education, as many as 12,000 to 14,000 people could be saved in 1991 from death by AIDS.

AIDS Will Impact All

The changes in our society will be economic and political and will affect our social institutions, our educational practices and our health care. Although AIDS may never touch you personally, the societal impact certainly will.

Be Educated—Be Prepared

Be prepared. Learn as much about AIDS as you can. Learn to separate scientific information from rumor and myth. The Public Health Service, your local public health officials and your family physician will be able to help you.

Concern About Spread of AIDS

While the concentration of AIDS cases is in the larger urban areas today, it has been found in every state and with the mobility of our society, it is likely that cases of AIDS will appear far and wide.

Special Educational Concerns

There are a number of people, primarily adolescents, that do not yet know they will be homosexual or become drug abusers and will not heed this message; there are others who are illiterate and cannot heed this message. They must be reached and taught the risk behaviors that expose them to infection with the AIDS virus.

High Risk Get Blood Test

The greatest public health problem lies in the large number of individuals with a history of high risk behavior who have been infected with and may be spreading the AIDS virus. Those with high risk behavior must be encouraged to protect others by adopting safe sexual practices and by the use of clean equipment for intravenous drug use. If a blood test for antibodies to the AIDS virus is necessary to get these individuals to use safe sexual practices, they should get a blood test. Call your local health department for information on where to get the test.

Anger and Guilt

Some people afflicted with AIDS will feel a sense of anger and others a sense of guilt. In spite of these understandable reactions, everyone must join the effort to control the epidemic, to provide for the care of those with AIDS, and to do all we can to inform and educate others about AIDS, and how to prevent it.

Confidentiality

Because of the stigma that has been associated with AIDS, many afflicted with the disease or who are infected with the AIDS virus are reluctant to be identified with AIDS. Because there is no vaccine to prevent AIDS and no cure, many feel there is nothing to be gained by revealing sexual contacts that might also be infected with the AIDS virus. When a community or a state requires reporting of those infected with the AIDS virus to public health authorities in order to trace sexual and intravenous drug contacts—as is the practice with other sexually transmitted diseases—those infected with the AIDS virus go underground out of the mainstream of health care and education. For this reason current public health practice is to protect the privacy of the individual infected with the AIDS virus and to maintain the strictest confidentiality concerning his/her health records.

State and Local AIDS Task Forces

Many state and local jurisdictions where AIDS has been seen in the greatest numbers have AIDS task forces with heavy representation from the field of public health joined by others who can speak broadly to issues of access to care, provision of care and the availability of community and psychiatric support services. Such a task force is needed in every community with the power to develop plans and policies, to speak and to act for the good of the public health at every level.

State and local task forces should plan ahead and work collaboratively with other jurisdictions to reduce transmission of AIDS by far-reaching informational and educational programs. As AIDS impacts more strongly on society, they should be charged with making recommendations to provide for the needs of those afflicted with AIDS. They also will be in the best position to answer the concerns and direct the activities of those who are not infected with the AIDS virus.

The responsibility of State and local task forces should be far reaching and might include the following areas:

■ Insure enforcement of public health regulation of such practices as ear piercing and tattooing to prevent transmission of the AIDS virus.

■ Conduct AIDS education programs for police, firemen, correctional institution workers and emergency medical personnel for dealing with AIDS victims and the public.

■ Insure that institutions catering to children or adults who soil themselves or their surroundings with urine, stool and vomitus have adequate equipment for cleanup and disposal, and have policies to insure the practice of good hygiene.

School

Schools will have special problems in the future. In addition to the guidelines already mentioned in this pamphlet, there are other things that should be considered such as sex education and education of the handicapped.

Sex Education

Education concerning AIDS must start at the lowest grade possible as part of any health and hygiene program. The appearance of AIDS could bring together diverse groups of parents and educators with opposing views on inclusion of sex education in the curricula. There is now no doubt that we need sex education in schools and that it must include information on heterosexual and homosexual relationships. The threat of AIDS should be sufficient to permit a sex education curriculum with a heavy emphasis on prevention of AIDS and other sexually transmitted diseases.

Handicapped and Special Education

Children with AIDS or ARC will be attending school along with others who carry the AIDS virus. Some children will develop brain disease which will produce changes in mental behavior. Because of the right to special education of the handicapped and the mentally retarded, school boards and higher authorities will have to provide guidelines for the management of such children on a case-by-case basis.

Labor and Management

Labor and management can do much to prepare for AIDS so that misinformation is kept to a minimum. Unions should issue preventive health messages because many employees will listen more carefully to a union message than they will to one from public health authorities.

AIDS Education at the Work Site

Offices, factories and other work sites should have a plan in operation for education of the work force and accommodation of AIDS or ARC patients *before* the first such case appears at the work site. Employees with AIDS or ARC should be dealt with as are any workers with a chronic illness. In-house video programs provide an excellent source of education and can be individualized to the needs of a specific work group.

Strain on the Health Care Delivery System

The health care system in many places will be overburdened as it is now in urban areas with large numbers of AIDS patients. It is predicted that during 1991 there will be 145,000 patients requiring hospitalization at least once and 54,000 patients who will die of AIDS. Mental disease (dementia) will occur in some patients who have the AIDS virus before they have any other manifestation such as ARC or classic AIDS.

State and local task forces will have to plan for these patients by utilizing conventional and time honored systems but will also have to investigate alternate methods of treatment and alternate sites for care including homecare.

The strain on the health system can be lessened by family, social and psychological support mechanisms in the community. Programs are needed to train chaplains, clergy, social workers and volunteers to deal with AIDS. Such support is particularly critical to the minority communities.

Mental Health

Our society will also face an additional burden as we better understand the mental health implications of infection by the AIDS virus. Upon being informed of infection with the AIDS virus, a young, active, vigorous person faces anxiety and depression brought on by fears associated with social isolation, illness and dying. Dealing with these individual and family concerns will require the best efforts of mental health professionals.

Controversial Issues

A number of controversial AIDS issues have arisen and will continue to be debated largely because of lack of knowledge about AIDS, how it is spread and how it can be prevented. Among these are the issues of compulsory blood testing, quarantine and identification of AIDS carriers by some visible sign.

Compulsory Blood Testing

Compulsory blood testing of individuals is not necessary. The procedure could be unmanageable and cost prohibitive. It can be expected that many who *test* negatively might actually be positive due to *recent* exposure to the AIDS virus and give a false sense of security to the individual and his/her sexual partners concerning necessary protective behavior. The prevention behavior described in this report, if adopted, will protect the American public and contain the AIDS epidemic. Voluntary testing will be available to those who have been involved in high risk behavior.

Quarantine

Quarantine has no role in the management of AIDS because AIDS is not spread by casual contact. The only time that some form of quarantine might be indicated is in a situation where an individual carrying the AIDS virus knowingly and willingly continues to expose others through sexual contact or sharing drug equipment. Such circumstances should be managed on a case-by-case basis by local authorities.

Identification of AIDS Carriers by Some Visible Sign

Those who suggest the marking of carriers of the AIDS virus by some visible sign have not thought the matter through thoroughly. It would require testing of the entire population, which is unnecessary, unmanageable and costly. It would miss those recently infected individuals who would test negatively, but be infected. The entire procedure would give a false sense of security. AIDS must and will be treated as a disease that can infect anyone. AIDS should not be used as an excuse to discriminate against any group or individual.

Updating Information

As the Surgeon General, I will continually monitor the most current and active health, medical and scientific information and make it available to you, the American people. Armed with this information you can join in the discussion and resolution of AIDS-related issues that are critical to your health, your children's health and the health of the nation.

Information Sources

U.S. Public Health Service
Public Affairs Office
Hubert H. Humphrey Bldg.
Room 725-H
200 Independence Ave., S.W.
Washington, D.C. 20201
(202) 245-6867

Local Red Cross or
American Red Cross AIDS
Education Office
1730 D St., N.W.
Washington, D.C. 20006
(202) 639-3223

Book List

The books listed here may provide additional help for you on the topics discussed in *Hot Buttons II*. Regal Books and Gospel Light Publications do not necessarily endorse the entire contents of all publications referred to in this list.

AIDS

Antonio, Gene. *The AIDS Cover-Up? The Real and Alarming Facts About AIDS*. San Francisco: Ignatius Press, 1986.

McKeever, Dr. James. *The AIDS Plague*. Medford: Omega Publications, 1986.

Coping with Trauma in the Home

General

Ahlem, Lloyd H. *Living with Stress*. Ventura: Regal Books, 1978.

Augsburger, David. *Caring Enough to Confront: The Love-Fight.* Ventura: Regal Books, 1974.

Sehnert, Keith W., M.D. *Stress/Unstress.* Minneapolis: Augsburg Publishing House, 1981.

Skoglund, Elizabeth. *Coping.* Ventura: Regal Books, 1979.

Timmons, Tim. *Stress in the Family: How to Live Through It.* Eugene: Harvest House Publications, 1982.

Incest

Edwards, Katherine. *A House Divided.* Grand Rapids: Zondervan Publishing House, 1984.

Janssen, Martha. *Silent Scream.* Philadelphia: Fortress Press, 1983.

Alcoholism

Costales, Claire and Barnack, Priscilla. *A Secret Hell: Surviving Life with an Alcoholic.* Ventura: Regal Books, 1984.

————— with Berry, Joe. *Staying Dry: A Workable Solution to the Problem of Alcohol Abuse,* rev. ed. Ventura: Regal Books, 1983.

Dunn, Jerry G. *God Is for the Alcoholic.* Chicago: Moody Press, 1967.

Wilkerson, David. *Sipping Saints.* Old Tappan: Fleming H. Revell Company, 1979.

Physical Abuse

Olson, Esther L. and Petersen, Kenneth. *No Place to Hide.* Wheaton: Tyndale Publishing House, 1982.

Death of a Loved One

Lewis, C.S. *A Grief Observed.* New York: Bantam Books, 1976.

Price, Eugenia. *Getting Through the Night: Finding Your Way After the Loss of a Loved One*. New York: Walker and Company, 1984.

Swindoll, Charles R. *For Those Who Hurt*. Portland: Multnomah Press, 1977.

Wiersbe, Warren W. *Why Us? When Bad Things Happen to God's People*. Old Tappan: Fleming H. Revell Company, 1983.

Living Together (Without Benefit of Marriage)

Burns, James. *Handling Your Hormones: The "Straight Scoop" on Love and Sexuality*. Laguna Hills: Merit Books.

Women and the Church

Evans, Mary J. *Women in the Bible*. Downers Grove: Inter-Varsity Press, 1983.

Malcolm, Kari Torgesen. *Women at the Crossroads*. Downers Grove: Inter-Varsity Press, 1982.

Interracial Relationships

Bigotry
Perkins, John M. *Let Justice Roll Down*. Ventura: Regal Books, 1976.

Tutu, Desmond. *Hope and Suffering: Sermons and Speeches*. Grand Rapids: William B. Eerdmans Publishing Company, 1984.

Marriage to Unbelievers
Lovett, C.S., *Unequally Yoked Wives*. Baldwin Park: Personal Christianity, 1968.

Mitchell, Marcia. *Spiritually Single*. Minneapolis: Bethany House Publishers, 1984.

Swearing

Montagu, Ashley. *The Anatomy of Swearing*. New York: The Macmillan Company, 1967.

Divorce

Adams, Jay E. *Marriage, Divorce, and Remarriage in the Bible*. Grand Rapids: Zondervan Publishing House, 1980.

Duty, Guy. *Divorce & Remarriage*. Minneapolis: Bethany House Publishers, 1967.

Smoke, Jim. *Living Beyond Divorce*. Eugene: Harvest House Publishers, 1984.

—————. *Growing Through Divorce*. Eugene: Harvest House Publishers, 1984.

Eating Disorders

Barrile, Jackie. *Confessions of a Closet Eater*. Wheaton: Tyndale Publishing House, 1983.

O'Neill, Cherry B. *Starving for Attention*. New York: Continuum, 1982.

Rowland, Cynthia. *Monster Within*. Grand Rapids: Baker Book House, 1985.

Thomas, Ann. *God's Answer to Overeating*. Lynnwood: Women's Aglow, 1975.

Suicide

Baucom, John Q. *Fatal Choice: The Teenage Suicide Crisis*. Chicago: Moody Press.

Blackburn, Bill. *What You Should Know About Suicide*. Waco: Word Books, 1982.

Hewett, John H. *After Suicide*. Philadelphia: Westminster Press, 1980.

Page, Carole Gift. *Neeley Never Said Goodbye*.

Chicago: Moody Press, 1984.

Authority in the Family

Getz, Gene A. *The Measure of a Family*. Ventura: Regal Books, 1976.

Narramore, Clyde M. *How to Succeed in Family Living*. Ventura: Regal Books, 1968.

Wakefield, Norm. *You Can Have a Happier Family*. Ventura: Regal Books, 1977.

Sexual Roles in Our Culture

Blitchington, W. Peter. *Sex Roles and the Christian Family*. Wheaton: Tyndale House Publishers, 1984.

————— and Evelyn. *Understanding the Male Ego*. Nashville: Thomas Nelson Publishers, 1984.

Elliot, Elizabeth. *The Mark of a Man*. Old Tappan: Fleming H. Revell, 1981.

Gene Getz, A. *The Measure of a Man*. Ventura: Regal Books, 1974.

————— *The Measure of a Woman*. Ventura: Regal Books, 1977.

Pagan Influences on Celebrations

Collins, Gary R. *Handling the Holidays*. Ventura: Regal Books, 1975.

General

Birch, Bruce C. and Rasmussen, Larry. *Bible and Ethics in the Christian Life*. Minneapolis: Augsburg Publishing House, 1976.

Chambers, Oswald. *Biblical Ethics.* Fort Washington: Christian Literature Crusade, 1964.

Stringfellow, William. *An Ethic for Christians and Other Aliens in a Strange Land.* Waco: Word Books, 1976.